Shavetail

The Odyssey of an Infantry Lieutenant in World War II

by

William L. Devitt

11/21/05.

To Dwight Saville

Best wishes from

a fellow veteran!

William L. Devitt

NORTH STAR PRESS OF ST. CLOUD, INC.

Library of Congress Cataloging-in-Publication Data

Devitt, William L., 1923-
   Shavetail : the odyssey of an infantry lieutenant in World War II / by
William L. Devitt.
      p. cm.
   Includes index.
   ISBN 0-87839-161-4 (alk. paper)
      1. Devitt, William L., 1923- 2. World War, 1939-1945—Personal
narratives, American. 3. United States. Army—Officers—Biography.
4. United States. Army. Infantry Regiment, 330th. E Company—History.
5. World War, 1939-1945—Regimental histories—United States. 6.
World War, 1939-1945—Campaigns—Western Front. 7. Hèrtgen, Battle
of, 1944. I. Title.

D811.D435 A3 2001
940.54'1273--dc21   2001030708

Author photo by Christopher Devitt.

First paperback edition, October 2003
Second printing, August 2005

ISBN: 0-87839-202-5 Paper
ISBN: 0-87839-161-4 Hardcover

Printed in the United States of America
by Versa Press, Inc., East Peoria, Illinois

Published by
North Star Press of St. Cloud, Inc.
P.O. Box 451
St. Cloud, Minnesota 56302

"Shavetail"—a newly commissioned officer: second lieutenant.
Usually used disparagingly.

Webster's Third New International Dictionary of the English Language, Unabridged

Dedication

To my friends and classmates of the St. Thomas Military Academy class of 1941, especially those who were killed in military service during World War II—Vince O'Connor, Glen Fadden, Frank Gearon, Jim Jago, Phil McGarry, and Richard Savoie—and further, to all the young men of E Company, 330th Infantry Regiment, 83rd Infantry Division, who served in Europe during the war.

Acknowledgements

My thanks to:

My oldest son, Chris, who typed the first draft years ago from my nearly undecipherable handwriting.

My niece and godchild, Patty Bard, and my second son, Sean, for reading and editing the text and for editing the final, final draft.

Sean, the first to encourage me to publish the book and his continuing help and encouragement.

My oldest daughter, Mary, for her review and comments, especially as to Chapter One.

My nephew Paul Bard, who edited an earlier draft word for word and whose sharp eye for detail helped greatly.

My third son, Nick, for his interest and suggestions.

My youngest son, Willy, for his interest in the subject matter and in me, as well as his comments.

My daughter Sarah (Dollie), the baby of the family (she'll like that), for her interest and suggestions.

My old and good friends and St. Thomas Academy classmates, Don Giefer and Al Luger, for their reading and commenting on the book.

Bub Huch, my grade school, high school, and college classmate and friend, for reading and commenting on the text and giving me the D-Day accounts contained in Appendices B and C. Sadly, Bob died in 2000.

Wally Kurtz, of St. Thomas Academy, for editing and commenting.

My friend Bill Etem, for his suggestions in regard to the section entitled "A Battle Outside the Bulge."

Shirley Johnson, Frank Chambers' daughter, for the use of several photographs.

Robert Derickson and the 83rd Infantray Division Association for permission to use numerous photographs.

Dr. Stephen E. Ambrose (of *Citizen Soldiers, Band of Brothers,* et al fame), for his interest and his suggestion to include "in World War II" in the subtitle.

John J. "Jack" Koblas, for reading the manuscript and rendering his sparkling review.

Jerry Rutkowski and his wife, Eileen, of Hopkins Secretarial Service, for their splendid work in typing and retyping the manuscript.

Rita, Corinne, and Seal Dwyer at North Star Press of St. Cloud, Inc., the publisher, for their help and encouragement.

My dear wife, Mary, for coming up with the title *Shavetail* and for her suggestions and patience through the entire exercise.

Table of Contents

Prologue

T HE SECOND WORLD WAR was the largest single event in human history . . ." wrote John Keegan in the Foreword to his book, *The Second World War*. This quotation reminds me that I participated in not just another war but in an historical event of unparalleled magnitude. I hope, then, that this book will be read not merely as another war story but as a perspective into one of the greatest of the world's dramas.

It follows that the most important event of my life was my participation in World War II. It took three years of my life and left me with memories and experiences that cannot be duplicated or forgotten. The memories, especially those of my experiences as a combat infantryman, are locked into my mind, and I cannot shake them. Those combat experiences, usually involving death or injury, continue to be replayed within me. There is no way to forget them even if I wanted to, and I don't. I keep going back fifty years to the days when I was young and was thrust into battle, thinking, or at least hoping, that I would live forever. Although, with the accuracy of the German artillery, mortar, and small arms fire, a long life was a hope not likely to be realized. Today as an old man, I realize that death might come at any time for either young or old.

I was an infantry lieutenant in the United States Army in Europe during World War II, and this is largely the story of what I saw and experienced in the army during the war. My time in combat was spent as a rifle platoon leader with E Company, 330th Infantry Regiment, 83rd Infantry Division. I am generally reporting only what I saw. There is, therefore, little comment on other units that were part of E Company's operations, or even on other platoons within E Company. As a lowly infantry lieutenant, I didn't get to see the big picture.

Although I was in combat, my combat experience was neither so long nor so comprehensive as that of many other infantrymen; therefore, there were gaps in my experience. For example, I participated in several attacks against the Germans, yet I was never subjected to one of their counterattacks, a hallmark of German defensive tactics.

I would like the reader to bear in mind the disproportionately high casualties suffered by the relatively small group I call front-line infantrymen, the great majority of whom were in rifle companies. Only about one out of every five soldiers was a front-line infantryman. Others were busy furnishing them with the support needed to do the fighting. They included signal (communications), transportation, medical, artillery, supply, ordinance, engineers, and more. Some who called themselves infantrymen—from division, regimental or battalion headquarters—were not what I consider front-line infantrymen, those who were constantly face to face with the enemy and lived with the ever-present risk of death or injury.

In an infantry division of 11,000 men, there were twenty-seven rifle companies of 190 men each, making a total of about 5,000 men in the rifle companies. There were also thousands of non-combat troops who were not assigned to divisions, being part of corps, army, or other commands. If the division reported casualties of thirty percent (3,300 men), those consisted largely of front line infantrymen—those in the rifle companies. That means that they suffered close to seventy percent (3,300 out of 5,000) killed and wounded. Many of them suffered well over one hundred percent casualties during the war. How? If all the men in a company became casualties (100 percent), replacements would come for them. If the replacements suffered fifty percent casualties, then the total casualties were 150 percent.

A major concern I had, and which I'm sure most young infantry officers had about themselves prior to first entering combat, was whether or not I had the training, ability, but most important, the courage to lead my men well. The fear of finding out, especially of being found out, that I was a coward and might run away or break down and cry in the midst of the battlefield turmoil was secreted in the back of my mind. I was able to overcome the crying obstacle, but I'll leave it to the reader to determine how well I managed the leadership question.

Introduction

M AY 8, 1945, VE DAY (Victory in Europe), is the day
World War II ended in Europe. I was a first lieutenant
in München-Gladbach, Germany, which happened to
be the hometown of Joseph Goebbels, Propaganda Minister of
the Third Reich. As one in a group of men going back to their
units, I was returning from a hospital in England. I was heading to my unit, the 83rd Division, which was near the Elbe River
in eastern Germany. We had stopped in München-Gladbach for
a day and night before moving on. At the moment when I heard
of the end of hostilities, I was walking in the street outside a
two-story apartment building we were using as a barracks. As
I walked toward the building, a shot was fired from a second
floor window, apparently in celebration of the news.

Since we were not in a combat area, no one was supposed to have ammunition, let alone fire it. So I, with the two
lieutenants with me, ran into the building to find the marks-
man. We went up to the second floor and entered a large room
where we found a dozen or so American soldiers, all of whom
had rifles.

I asked who had fired the shot and, not surprisingly,
received no affirmative reply. I immediately started to feel the
barrel of each rifle, and soon found one barrel which was hot—
the weapon of the man who had fired the shot.

The poor fellow was told that we couldn't allow men to discharge their rifles randomly for fear of an accident. I don't think that I convinced him, a combat veteran, of the correctness of my position, but he was not disciplined further, and the incident was closed.

This is the story of my experiences in getting from my hometown of Saint Paul, Minnesota, to München-Gladbach, Germany.

Chapter One

In the United States and England
September 1937 to July 1944

ORTY DIRTY, UNSHAVEN, dead-tired young American infantrymen walked single file up a hill out of the little German town of Untermaubach where they had spent the last four days attacking the Wehrmacht infantry. It was over for now. The town was on the edge of the Hürtgen Forest. These Americans had been fighting at that location for over three weeks and had not shaved nor bathed nor changed clothing in that time. They carried the memories of the 150 other men of the company who had entered the forest with them and had been killed or wounded by the fierce German resistance.

It was Christmas Eve of 1944, and the forty survivors were happy to be alive. But their happiness was tempered by the realization that as soon as the company received replacements for their fallen comrades, they would be at it again. At the head of the column was the company commander, the third since entering the Hürtgen. At the rear was the other surviving officer in the company, a tall, skinny, twenty-one-year-old second lieutenant with steel-rimmed, army-issued glasses. I was that lieutenant.

St. Thomas Military Academy

My participation in World War II or, more accurately, the nature or kind of my participation, came about by happenstance. I went to a high school that had a Reserve Officers

Training Corps (ROTC) program, which entitled me to a commission as an infantry second lieutenant at the outbreak of the war. Without the ROTC, I might have been lucky and ended up in the army folding clothes in a post laundry.

My school was St. Thomas Military Academy (now St. Thomas Academy) in St. Paul, Minnesota. I graduated in 1941. The happenstance I mentioned was that my parents didn't send my two brothers and me to St. Thomas because of the military training but rather because it was a highly regarded Catholic school within walking distance of our home.

At St. Thomas, we drilled and marched five days a week and had two hours per week of military classroom work. We studied infantry tactics, first aid and sanitation, weapons (including machine guns, rifles, and mortars), and a myriad of other military subjects. This was in addition to the usual courses, which, for freshmen, included English, Latin, algebra, history, and religion.

The army used our time badly at St. Thomas. A more sensible allocation would have been five hours per week of military subjects, and two hours of drill. We spent endless hours in close-order drill, marching back and forth in different sized units, attempting to make various maneuvers in unison such as a right face or a left turn. We were like a militarized version of can-can dancers in a Paris dance hall. Close order drill might have had an important place in the training of can-can dancers or the Radio City Music Hall Rockettes but had little to do with the skills necessary for an infantryman in combat.

Although we studied infantry tactics, I don't think that any of our instructors had any first-hand knowledge of infantry combat. Our PMS&T (Professor of Military Science and Tactics), Lieutenant Colonel Burton Hood, talked about the "fog of war." He'd say, "Now you cadets should realize that when the field manual states that one platoon will conduct a frontal attack and one platoon will perform a flanking movement to hit the enemy's right or left flank, things don't always turn out the way they're planned. There's something called the 'fog of war.' That means there's always confusion in battle.

The Academy building, built in the nineteenth century, was where the students of St. Thomas Military Academy attended classes. This picture was taken from the 1941 edition of the school's yearbook, the *Kaydet*. The building was on the campus of the College of St. Thomas, now the University of St. Thomas, in St. Paul, Minnesota. The far left side of the building appears to be headed uphill. That must be some sort of photographic error. I'm sure my classmates from the Class of '41 will agree that we were always "on the level" at school. Years ago, the Academy moved off the campus to another site. In the true American tradition that newer is better, the Academy building was torn down for, I presume, something newer. So, in this year 2001, the sixtieth anniversary of our graduation, we, the remaining members of the Class of '41, will not be able to revisit any classroom except in our memories. (Photo provided by the author)

Sometimes there is so much confusion that everything seems to go wrong. At other times, there is so little disorder that things just turn out right. For example, if the company commander sends a messenger to the flanking platoon leader to commence the assault and the messenger is killed or wounded on the way, the platoon leader doesn't get the message and nothing happens."

The reader should understand that all the dialogue in this story took place over fifty years ago. Although everything said is to the best of my recollection, time tends to make the exact wording hazy and uncertain.

No one talked of the killing and dying that were part of battle nor of the fear that soldiers felt. No one discussed how a young officer should handle a combat situation in which he had to decide which of two severely wounded men he should order to be evacuated first from the battlefield, one wounded in both legs but able to talk and plead to be taken first and the second unconscious from a deep shrapnel wound in his chest. Nor did we ever consider the paralyzing terror and mindless hysteria that overtook a man so that he could not get off the ground and run to the relative safety of a foxhole when shells were exploding all around him. Unlike my military instructors at St. Thomas, I experienced both of these situations while in combat in Germany in 1944. Although we learned much in training about military life, my impression of combat from the perspective of a high school student, was that it wasn't particularly terrifying. When I faced enemy fire in Europe in 1944, I discovered quite the contrary. High school was never like that.

During the summer before my sophomore year, the entire school spent a few weeks at Camp Ripley in northern Minnesota. We lived in tents and had a chance to fire on the rifle range, eat in a mess hall, and get a feeling for army life. On the rifle range, we fired the M1903 Springfield rifle used by the U.S. Army in World War I. The Springfield was a .30 caliber weapon that produced a powerful kick when fired. After firing the rifle, most of us ended up with a swollen lip. This happened because we failed to hold the rifle firmly against the shoulder, thereby causing the kick to force the right hand (and thumb) backward, striking the right side of the lip, which immediately swelled up to twice its size. As we, just boys, walked around camp quite proud of our swollen right lips, we thought that this was a mark of our oncoming manhood. It was really a sign of our ineptitude in handling the rifle.

In the summer before our senior year (when I was seventeen years old) we spent six weeks at Fort Snelling, near Saint Paul. That, together with our time at Camp Ripley, was our only experience in an army camp before being called to active duty as second lieutenants after the war began. When I arrived at my first army assignment, I had never been through basic training and in many ways knew little more about the army than some of the new recruits I was about to instruct on how to be a soldier. It was like the nearly blind leading the blind.

Most of the fellows at Fort Snelling were juniors in college. We, the St. Thomas boys, were the only trainees of high school age. One day we had an inspection in which we were required to lay out all of our equipment, even our toiletries. When the inspecting officer came to me he noted that I had no razor.

"Where's your razor, son?" he asked.

"I don't have one, sir," I replied.

"What do you mean, you don't have one? How do you shave?"

"Well, sir, you see, I don't shave."

Since the only shaving I'd had to do at that age was the occasional snip with my father's razor, I had no need for one of my own. The officer stared at me in disbelief for a second, and then turned away without saying a word, probably thinking, "What is this man's army coming to?"

Four and one-half years later, I was fighting in Germany in one of the bloodiest battles of the war—in the Hürtgen Forest. Daily, often hourly, we were subjected to intense German artillery, mortar, or small arms fire. We spent much of the time hugging the ground or diving into and cringing in log covered foxholes. As a result, I had gone for three weeks without shaving and had grown a scraggly beard and a mustache, which ran from light to dark brown, together with some almost bare patches. I decided to shave the beard and let the mustache grow to something that might have been halfway decent looking. After about a month of additional growth, I realized that I needed more years on my body to qualify for a real mustache, so I shaved it off.

World War II started in September 1939, after the Germans invaded Poland. The Germans, with help from the Russians, finished off the Poles in about a month. The period between the Polish defeat and April 1940 was known as the "Phony War." The Germans and the French sat behind their border defenses like ocean-front homeowners battened down and awaiting the onslaught of a hurricane. They did little fighting until the Germans commenced their "blitzkrieg." Within weeks, the Germans had overwhelmed the French, British, Belgians, Dutch, Norwegians, and Danes.

At St. Thomas, we kept up with all the developments in the war and hoped and prayed for the Allies to succeed, but I don't think I ever speculated as to what effect an American entry into the war might have on me. Although St. Thomas was a military school, I don't recall the instructors bringing the war into the school curriculum. For the two years and three months between the beginning of the war and Pearl Harbor, I was very curious as to how American troops would do in combat. I was sure that we would win any battle no matter what the enemy did. History showed me to be a poor prophet.

The United States entered the war on December 7, 1941, when the Japanese attacked Pearl Harbor in Hawaii and dealt a crippling blow to the American naval forces.

December seventh was a Sunday, and our family heard the news over the radio about noon, soon after we had returned home from Mass. My sister's boyfriend, Bob Moberg, had come over to the house for lunch, and when he heard the news, I overheard him exclaim, "Those dirty yellow bastards!"

His reaction was not uncommon; it was the feeling of many Americans that the Japanese were sneaky and perhaps unsportsmanlike for having attacked us without warning or a declaration of war, especially since the Japanese had a special envoy in Washington discussing with Secretary of State Cordell Hull possible ways of reducing the tension between the two countries. I didn't feel that way about the Japanese at the time, and I certainly don't now. My feeling is that since they were determined to attack us, they did so in the way that gave them the best chance for success. War is a life-and-death thing and is not governed by rules of etiquette.

After we entered the war, the recruiting offices filled with young men wanting to fight the Germans and Japanese. The recruiting offices were packed as if it were a Sear's one-day sale. I didn't feel any great onrush of patriotism. I was in my first year of college and hoped to finish the school year. I expected to get my commission as a second lieutenant, so I was in no hurry to get into the fray.

Many of my classmates, as well as myself, were called to active duty as second lieutenants in 1942, and since most fellows my age expected to be going into military service, I was ready to go. When I took the physical exam, the doctors said I had a heart murmur. Upon further examination, it was decided that I didn't. It was February 1943. I was nineteen.

Camp Robinson

In early March 1943, I boarded a train in Saint Paul to go to Camp Joseph T. Robinson just outside Little Rock, Arkansas. To me, this was the trip of a lifetime. I was a child of the Depression—I had never before been outside Minnesota, and I had certainly never been to the South.

To the sophisticated and well-traveled young Americans of the 1990s, this would have been no big deal. But to me, it was like a trip to a far-off country such as Tibet, except that in the South they spoke a language quite similar to mine, and to which I soon became accustomed.

My mother had this choirboy-like picture taken of me soon after I was called to active duty in 1943. It's hard to believe that this less-than-war-like, nineteen-year old only two years later would be trying to end the lives of others the same age who happened to be in the German army.

My friend and classmate Neil Gallagher was on the train with me. When we got off the train in Little Rock, we noted immediately one difference between Saint Paul and the South. In the railroad station, we saw signs for drinking fountains and toilets that read "White Only" and "Colored Only." This was our first view of official segregation, and we were startled and puzzled by it. We were not flaming liberals, but we were struck by the innate unfairness and degradation associated with segregation.

We got into the taxi meant to take us out to Camp Robinson. Because of the wartime transportation shortage, we were joined by two or three businessmen who were to be dropped off somewhere in Little Rock. They were dressed in suits and ties, were obviously Southerners, and were considerably older than we. Since it was fresh on my mind, I mentioned the signs in the station.

"Why do you have drinking fountains marked 'White' and 'Colored'? I've never seen such a thing. What's going on?"

"Listen," said one of them, "Ya'll better watch your talk. How we run our lives is none of your damn business. Ya'll don't have to live with the Nigras, but we do. Ya'll don't know anything about our problems, but ya'll want to tell us how to live."

"I wasn't trying to tell you anything," I said. "This is all new to me. It's my first day here. I've never been out of Minnesota before. Say, what do the Negroes think about those signs?"

"It's none of your Goddamn business what we do here. We get along fine with our Nigras. I'll tell you, son, ya'll get along a damn site better if ya'll keep your damn mouth shut. You're in Arkansas now, and ya'll better let us handle our own affairs."

I suppose that my commenting on their way of life as soon as I arrived in town seemed to them to be rather rude. Yet I merely said what I thought and felt.

Not only was segregation the rule in Little Rock, but it also was the rule throughout the entire United States Army.

Being with all-white troops did not seem surprising to me since I was raised in a lily-white society in which the few blacks in St. Paul lived largely in one area, on or close to Rondo Street, near downtown, and we had little occasion to see them. The only black person I saw with any regularity was our postman, whom we called "Colonel." When he'd bring the mail to our front door, he would do so with a pleasant smile or a kindly remark.

The speech and racial customs were not the only things that were different in the South. The Southerners even had different foods. I remember my first meeting with a Little Rock girl who said, "Ya'll have to come over some time and try my Mama's grits and chitlins."

I didn't know whether she was talking about food or furniture. I later learned that grits look like Cream of Wheat cereal and that chitlins (also called chitterlings) are a food prepared from the intestines of pigs. Perhaps that daughter of the deep South and the Confederacy was trying to wreak some revenge on her damnyankee acquaintance.

Camp Robinson was a basic training camp, and I was a member of the cadre whose job was to train recruits into infantrymen. The only problem was that I didn't know much about the army. I had never been through basic training myself. To use an old army saying, "I didn't know shit from Shinola."

As soon as I arrived at the camp, I was assigned to a training company and was told to report to the company commander in the orderly room the next morning. An orderly room was the company headquarters. It was a small building, consisting of a large room that housed the company records and equipment. It was presided over by the first sergeant, aided by the company clerk and one or two other men. Beyond the large room would be another, the company commander's office. The junior officers didn't rate an office or even a desk. We'd hang out in the first sergeant's room, being careful not to get in his way.

I had never been in an orderly room before, so that first morning I approached the building with trepidation. I didn't know what to expect. What I saw did not surprise me, but what I heard gave me the shock of my young life. When I walked in, I met the first sergeant, an old regular army man. He was quite bald, and the arrangement of what little hair he had on his head reminded me of a monk's tonsure. But that was his only similarity to a monk. His vocabulary consisted of profanity interspersed with just enough non-profane words to convey some meaning to what he said.

I was raised in a household in which even the mildest forms of profanity were not used, not by my father, mother, two brothers, sister, nor myself. The strongest language in my family came from my mother who, from time to time, upon reaching the end of her patience, would exclaim, exasperated, "Oh, sugar!" My friends might occasionally have dropped a "hell" or a "damn" and in extreme circumstances let fly a "shit," but swearing was a rare ingredient in my life.

At my initial meeting with the first sergeant, he made my friends sound like bush leaguers in the profanity game. He was telling one of his men, "You tell those mother fuckin' recruits that I don't want no mother fuckin' excuses for not changing the mother fuckin' sheets on their mother fuckin' beds."

He seemed to use that quaint phrase at least once or twice in each sentence, and I think that he would have been speechless without it. I was stunned. I didn't know that such vile talk existed. It might be said that I had just become the ungrateful beneficiary of a speed course in foul language.

I was eating lunch in the mess hall one day with several of the non-coms when one of the sergeants asked me something about firing mortars. I had never fired a mortar nor had ever seen one fired.

I wish I had said something like:

"Sergeant, I've never fired a mortar, so I'm not the one to ask about mortars. You men probably don't know, but I got an ROTC commission only three months ago. We spent a lot of time in the classroom, but not much time out in the field with weapons like mortars. So I'm going to keep my eyes open and my mouth shut. Why don't you ask me a question on something I know about, like how many cities are there in the Twin Cities."

Rather than admit that I knew little about mortars, I gave the sergeant a noncommittal answer, "That's a good question, but I don't know the answer. I'll have to think about it."

After having been in combat, I learned the difference between the garrison and combat armies. When I first got to Camp Robinson, the company commander, a captain, was taking inventory of all the equipment in the company, and he assigned me the task of counting and listing the kitchenware.

"Devitt," he said, "I want you to be specially careful in counting the silverware. That's what we usually lose the most of. It's been six months since the last inventory, and I sure as hell don't want to be paying for a lot of silver because you can't count straight."

Although the captain had never been in combat, I'm sure he knew that a company in battle didn't need a full complement of silverware to advance against the enemy.

When I got into combat, the emphasis changed. We lost equipment, including the weapons of the killed and wounded, almost daily. Our concern was that we retained the most important equipment in order to do the job. If the man who carried the automatic rifle were killed or wounded, another man would discard his M-1 rifle and pick up the fallen man's weapon.

Fort Benning

After a couple of months at Camp Robinson, I was sent to the Infantry School at Fort Benning, Georgia to take the basic course for infantry lieutenants and captains. The course was similar to that given officer candidates, who were enlisted men being tested and trained to be officers. Our course was tailored for junior officers to be sure that they learned all of the basic elements of military life necessary to do their job.

One of the things we learned was how to pay a social visit to the commanding officer of the regiment upon first reporting for duty. The officer who instructed us did so in a lighthearted manner so that we realized that this was the least important subject presented to us at Benning.

"Gentlemen," he said, "You've probably heard there's a war going on. I've heard the same thing. So when I got the assignment to teach a bunch of infantry officers how to make a social visit, I thought they must have been kidding. I told the colonel that there must be better ways of making you people combat ready. The colonel said he agreed, so he went to the general and said that the students would probably laugh the instructor out of the classroom if he tried to teach the technicalities of a social visit. The general said he agreed too, but that that course had been taught at Benning for the last twenty-five years, and he wasn't about to change it now. This whole thing reminds me of the old army saying, 'There's the right way, and then there's the Army way.' Anyway, laugh all you want."

Then he explained how to make the social visit. The new second lieutenant would call upon the colonel and his wife at their quarters. The most important part of the visit was to leave your calling card on a table in the entry hall without being detected. Why? Our instructor didn't tell us. Now the colonel and his wife knew the calling card routine, so while they pretended not to be looking, the lieutenant would pull a card out of his pocket, back up to the table and slide the card onto it, like a fellow leaving a one-dollar tip for a fifty-dollar dinner, all the while carrying on an animated conversation. He would then walk into the living room as though nothing had happened.

Many of the students at Benning were ROTC graduates, such as myself, and were receiving their first experience in some of the military subjects. Others were experienced men who had many years in the army. For ROTC people, this could have been considered our basic training.

The following indicates how little I knew or how naive I was. We were out in the field for night maneuvers, and the instructor said to us, "When we get to the Harmony Church area, that's about three miles, we'll drop our rolls."

I was puzzled at what he meant. I thought to myself, "What are you talking about? No one gave me any rolls before, during, or after dinner, but I could eat a couple right now. But why would I want to drop them? I wonder if I should ask him what he means?"

Fortunately, I didn't embarrass myself by telling the instructor that I had no rolls. Eventually I learned that he was talking about dropping the bedrolls we were carrying.

While at Benning, we spent part of the time in the field, living in pup tents. Two pieces of canvas, called shelter halves, were buttoned together to form the complete unit. It was long enough to accommodate two men lying down side by side and barely high enough to sit up. Each man carried a shelter half as part of his gear and then teamed with his buddy or partner to make up the tent.

One evening we went out on a night exercise. It was dark when we got back to our tents, which were laid randomly in a wooded area. Before leaving the bivouac area for the exercise, we placed our bedrolls on the ground inside the tents so that we could get right into them upon our return. After I returned, as I was getting into my bedroll, a piercing shriek came from someone nearby. We all rushed out of our tents to see what had happened. The shrieker was standing outside of his tent, looking back toward it. As he was getting into his bedroll, he discovered that it was already occupied—by a snake. In the part of Georgia in which Fort Benning was situated, there were poisonous snakes, including the deadly water moccasin. No one noticed the type of snake that visited our friend, but after this incident we all used our flashlights to examine our bedrolls carefully before settling in for the night.

Benning was not all grim attention to duty and sober classroom work. One wag in our barracks put up a sign over the front entry, a take off the infantry motto, "Follow me." His new motto over the door read, "After you."

We also had a school song using the names of two streams that flowed through the Ft. Benning Military Reservation. It parodied the Cornell University song, "High Above Cayuga's Waters":

"High above the Chatahoochie lies the Upatoi.
Hail to thee our Alma Mater, Benning School for Boys."

Camp Shelby and the Hospital

After Fort Benning I was sent to Camp Shelby, Mississippi, to help train the men in a new division being formed, the 65th Infantry Division. Fortunately, I was much better prepared than I had been prior to Benning.

When I arrived at Shelby, I became part of the cadre of the 65th. The cadre consisted of the officers, non-commissioned officers, and other enlisted men—all of whom formed the nucleus of the division and would be in charge of training. The trainees, new recruits, were not to arrive for two or three weeks, so the cadre was divided into platoons for the purpose of doing refresher training while awaiting the arrival of the trainees.

I was assigned to a platoon consisting entirely of first and second lieutenants. Part of our time was spent in close-order drill, marching back and forth over a drill field. Each man in the platoon was assigned as platoon leader for part of a day. Most of the men did not take the training very seriously, so there was quite a bit of sloppy marching in the close-order drill. Since we were all lieutenants, we were accustomed to giving the drill orders rather than receiving them. Often the lieutenants would be out of step, and the crisp turns for right and left face demanded of trainees were largely ignored. All of this appalled me. The military subject I knew best was close-order drill. That was the only maneuver we performed daily at St. Thomas. My military education there might have been short on tactics and weaponry, but close-order drill was another story. During my four years at St. Thomas, we drilled every day. In addition we had frequent parades and also ceremonies for special occasions such as graduations and federal inspections.

My fairly foggy recollection of the field manual is that it called for the position of attention to be: heels on line together, feet spread equally at an angle of 45 degrees, knees straight without stiffness, hips level, stomach in, chest lifted and arched, shoulders level, arms hanging naturally with the thumbs along the seams of the trousers, and head and eyes straight to the front.

When my turn as platoon leader came, I told myself I'd put an end to the "disgraceful" drilling. When I called "Platoon attention," they acted just like what they were, a bunch of lowly lieutenants being commanded by a comrade of equal rank. To state it mildly, they were unenthusiastic. Some slowly put their heels together in the attention position. Rather than having head and eyes to the front as prescribed in the field manual, many looked to their left and right like spectators at a tennis match. Those were the good ones. The majority just ignored my order and continued their conversations with their neighbors.

I was not deterred. "All right, gentlemen" I said. "I'm going to call you to attention again, and I expect you to behave like soldiers, not girl scouts." That swipe at their manhoods had little effect. When I gave the command, "Platoon, attention," the reaction was about the same as before.

What now? I thought. *I'll show 'em. I'll wake 'em up. A few right, left, and about faces should do it.*

In my best "second lieutenant" authoritarian voice, I proclaimed loudly, "Ri-ight face." The reaction was not what I had hoped. Instead of the crisp face to the right in unison, the by now unhappy lieutenants, all faced to the right but about as far out of sync as thirty men could be.

I followed up with several more left, right, and about face commands. The response of the men became more lethargic with each movement. I was losing ground. Who was to win the battle? The mean, uncooperative "trainee" lieutenants, or the earnest, righteous, dimwitted platoon leader?

As my last hurrah, I thought instead of giving facing movements in quick succession I would march the platoon and give them "to the rear, march" movements one after another so quickly that they wouldn't have time to frustrate the platoon leader.

I would start them off marching in a column of threes and then order, "To the rear, march," "To the rear, march," "To the rear march," all in fairly rapid succession. As soon as they reversed in response to the first command and taken two or three steps in the opposite direction, the second command would require them to reverse themselves to the original direction. The third command would send them again to the opposite direction. I thought that the plan would make the men realize who was in charge and possibly make them feel that they had done a good job in successfully completing the maneuver.

I was beginning to perceive that I was not dealing with a crack drill platoon that practiced every day to ensure unison in its movements.

The plan had a less rosy result than I anticipated. Remember, these men were out of practice in marching as a group. It was probably months or even years since most of them had marched like this. Possibly, never.

The first "To the rear, march," went okay. The second, which almost immediately followed the first, found several men turning to the rear and finding the chest of the man following him driving into him like a blocking back on a football team. The third command merely completed the disaster. At the end there were nearly as many men on the ground as on their feet. Hollywood could not have designed a more disoriented, yet laughable, scene. There were men lying flat on their backs, some slowly arising and dusting themselves off, some staggering from the impact with a fellow soldier, and others rubbing their foreheads where the front edge of the fiber helmet liners of other men collided with them.

Most of the light weight helmet liners we were wearing had fallen off and were rolling on the ground like M&Ms from a package spilled on a slippery kitchen floor.

Fortunately there were no injuries. I'm sure all the men in the platoon were thinking, "What the hell is that idiot trying to prove?" Today I wonder the same thing. To use a favorite adjective, my behavior was "inexplicable."

But all's well that ends well. One of the supervising officers came over and told us that we were through with close-order drill for the day. He didn't question me about the incident, so I did not have to attempt to give an explanation of why it happened. I have not as yet figured out what I should have said, but I believe I should have included both humor and wisdom together with a touch of humility. Lots of humility.

At Camp Shelby I hurt my knee in a training accident and spent seven months in a hospital near Jackson, Mississippi. The injury occurred while walking along an old dirt road on a night maneuver. I stepped into a deep rut and twisted my right knee. Somehow bone and cartilage came loose under my kneecap so that I couldn't bend the knee.

After the accident, I did not immediately report my injury. I was reluctant to leave since I wanted to stay in the division and become part of a combat unit. The day after the accident, I felt a piece of bone or cartilage pop out from under the kneecap. I reached down and pushed it back in place. This condition continued, and for the next few days I pushed the piece back into place several times.

About the fourth day I was going up a stairway and fell forward, catching myself before I hit the stairs. The piece had lodged in the knee joint preventing the knee from bending. I got to my feet and fiddled with the knee a little and got it to work again. I then discovered that if I held my hand securely on the knee cap as I went up or down the stairs, the movement of the piece back into the joint would not occur. The next day or two things went all right. If as I walked along, the piece would pop out, I would reach down and push it into place. Whenever I walked up or down stairs, I would hold the knee and nothing would happen. Someone might ask if I had planned to play the knee game for the rest of my life. It should be no surprise to learn that I had no plans beyond how to negotiate the next flight of stairs.

A week or so after the accident, as I started down the stairway outside the barracks, my right knee wouldn't bend and I experienced a sharp pain. I fell forward to the ground at the foot of the short flight of stairs. I had forgot to hold the knee. I was not injured, but apparently the fall drove enough sense into my head to report to the medics who promptly sent me to the hospital for an operation.

Although the knee injury, operation, and hospitalization were not experiences I'd recommend to anyone, they brought about one happy result. The delay in getting back to duty possibly saved my life in that I was not sent overseas in time for the Allied invasion on D-Day and thus avoided the deadly fighting in Normandy and Brittany.

My longtime friend and St. Thomas classmate, Bob Huch, was not lucky enough to have missed D-Day. He landed on Omaha Beach as a section leader in the first wave with E company, 16th Infantry, 1st Infantry Division. They faced the most determined German resistance on the most heavily defended terrain in the invasion. Bob was one of the few men in his company who advanced off the beach. That day his company, with an original complement of 183 men, suffered 112 killed plus many wounded, a far greater death rate than suffered by Pickett's division at Gettysburg, eighty years earlier. Compared to D-Day, my pain-filled knee experience was a walk in the park.

I was sent to Foster General Hospital near Jackson where an operation removed the offending bone and cartilage fragments. In those days the practice was to avoid using the injured limb for a considerable period of time. Therefore, for the first month or two after the operation, I lay in bed with my leg attached to a weight connected to a metal frame. All day long, I would pull on a rope, which raised the weight, and I would then gradually release the rope, causing the weight to

Lieutenant Bob Huch, taken in Sicily in 1943. My good friend and class-mate in grade school, high school, and college. This rather peaceful and harmless-looking twenty-year old was a front-line infantryman in North Africa (1943), in Sicily (1943), on the first wave on Omaha Beach on D-Day (1944), and in all of northern Europe (1944 and 1945), including Normandy, Aachen, the Hürtgen Forest, the Battle of the Bulge and beyond. I have never heard of anyone else who was "up front" so long and survived—an unsung but true American hero. (Courtesy of Bob's sister, Irene Hartnett)

bend the knee, preventing it from getting stiff from inactivity. Today doctors would have the patient up and walking in a day or two.

After I was allowed out of bed, I remained in the hospital doing physical therapy but mostly just goofing off. Since I was an infantryman and not able to walk well, the army apparently felt that the hospital was the place for me to be, even though I was quite healthy except for a slight limp.

I was in a ward with about forty officers, all lieutenants and most of us in our early twenties. Since we were all orthopedic cases, we had little to do but go to the physical therapy department once or twice a day. We, therefore, had to devise ways to occupy our time. One of our most important activities was to bedevil the head nurse, a first lieutenant, who was in charge of our ward.

One morning someone said to her, "Lieutenant, the colonel's coming down the hall toward the ward. It looks like an inspection, and some of the beds aren't made. I wonder what he'll say?"

Without looking up or saying anything, her face turned pale, and she started to straighten the covers on the nearest bed. She then stopped and looked out into the hall and saw that the colonel was not there. We all laughed, and she said, "You know that isn't at all funny. I don't know why you behave like this. You act like a bunch of kids. Now go and make your beds."

We often teased her, but our greatest threat to her authority was sleeping late in the morning. She would plead with us to get out of bed and when that didn't work, she would threaten to report us to our superiors. Finally, when all else failed, she would rely on tears in the hope of stirring us, but we were not easily stirred, especially while in bed trying to get a few extra winks.

Every few days, while I would be dozing in my bed, one of my "buddies" in the ward, after getting the attention of the others, would quietly approach my bed and raise the weight on my leg a few inches and then let it drop. Next came my cry of pain followed immediately by the cheers and laughter of my fellow invalids who must have had mindsets similar to those of the bloodthirsty onlookers at the guillotine in the French Revolution. I was not amused.

During World War II, the army followed the indefensible practice of racial segregation. Although there were about forty of us in the ward, there was one lieutenant who had a private room. He was black. It seemed to me at the time that this was a strange situation in which the supposedly inferior black man was given better treatment than the supposedly superior white men. In truth the black lieutenant probably deserved better accommodations, because he was superior to us in most ways. He was from a northern city, Philadelphia, and had graduated in chemistry from a prestigious university. He was bright, well spoken, mature, and probably a better person than most of the forty of "us." I suspect that in Philadelphia he did not face this kind of officially sanctioned discrimination.

One day, soon after I was allowed to be out of bed, I received a pass to go into downtown Jackson. Upon getting on the public bus, I received a culture shock similar to the one that occurred in the train station in Little Rock. Although I don't recall any signs directing them to do so, all of the black people went to the rear of the bus.

I wish now that I had joined them as a protest, but I didn't. I remember wondering how the lieutenant from Philadelphia felt and reacted upon being faced with such unjust treatment. Here again I wish that I had talked to him, telling him that I was appalled by it, but, since I was fairly shy, I did not.

Fort McClellan

After getting out of the hospital, I was assigned to another training camp at Fort McClellan, Alabama. There I instructed recruits in various subjects, including the bayonet and the sixty millimeter mortar. By that time, I had learned something about mortars but not enough. As will be seen later, I failed to learn how to duck shrapnel from a mortar shell. But then there were few classes in ducking.

I had received little or no bayonet training at St. Thomas, Fort Snelling, or Camp Ripley. What I learned and remembered about it came from the Infantry School at Fort Benning. The bayonet, as used in the American army in World War II, was a double bladed knife about a foot long attached to the barrel of the M-1 rifle. It's ostensible purpose was to thrust into the enemy, either while attacking or defending. I always thought that using such a weapon on the enemy would be unnecessary, since, it seemed to me, it would be much simpler merely to shoot him. I think that the bayonet was a carry-over from the days of the single shot rifle, when the soldier would not have time to reload but instead used the blade to finish off his foes.

The real reasons bayonets were used in World War II were, I believe, first, that they had been used in World War I and earlier wars, so tradition was a factor. Second, it gave men in combat the feeling that they had another weapon to use, hence their morale and confidence increased. Finally, it was expected to terrify the enemy, causing them to surrender, run away, or to stop fighting. I don't know whether or not the latter two reasons were accurate, but any soldier would be happy to have anything that could possibly help repel an enemy in battle. Since I was an officer, I did not carry the M-1 rifle but instead carried the smaller carbine, which did not have a bayonet. I don't know why the army had junior officers carry the lighter carbine instead of the M-1, which weighed nine pounds. When I got into combat, I switched to the M-1, mainly so that I would not be identified by the enemy as an officer. Since I didn't carry a bayonet, I didn't attach one to my M-1, but the enlisted men, who had bayonets, usually had one affixed to the M-1 while in combat. However, the only times I saw them used in combat was for opening "C" ration cans. (See Appendix A for a description of bayonet drill.)

I was at Fort McClellan on June 6, 1944, D-Day in Europe. We had all been expecting the invasion. The Russians had been clamoring for the last two years for an invasion by the Allies, and the newspapers and radio were increasingly predicting that it would come in 1944. When I heard the news, I was happy that the long delayed invasion had come and with it the expectation of a closer end to the war. One of my friends said to me, "What d'ya think of the news?"

"I'm glad," I replied. "We all knew it was coming. I just hope they can hold on to that beachhead when the Germans counterattack. What do you think?"

"Oh," he said. "They'll be needing plenty of replacements. I'll bet we'll all get orders soon. We won't stay here much longer."

The prospect of combat did not disturb me especially, probably because I didn't realize how unbelievably terrorizing it could be. Besides, I was young and foolish and curious as to what lay ahead of me. I had thought that once the Allied forces landed in Europe I would be sent there. The army did not disappoint me. Shortly after D-Day, I was sent to Camp Shanks, outside of New York City, for processing to be sent to Europe. At Camp Shanks, we got gas masks, clothing, and medical checkups, including immunization shots. I was one of a large group of company-grade officers (captains and lieutenants) who were replacements for the officers who had been casualties during and after the landings in France.

To England

We traveled in an Australian troopship, which was part of a large convoy. This was my first time in a vessel larger than a Mississippi River steamboat.

The trip took about twelve days from New York to Liverpool. My most vivid recollection of the crossing was the contrast between the officers' accommodations and those of the enlisted men. The officers, even low-ranking second lieutenants such as myself, slept in cabins with bunks and sheets and pillow cases. I was in a cabin with three other lieutenants, and we had an attendant who made our beds and cleaned the cabins. "Boy, this is the life," I said. "Someone to make the beds and pick up the room. If my mother saw this, she

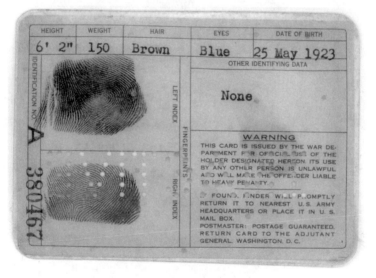

My ID card issued at Camp Shanks, New York, just prior to leaving for England. Note the date. My grim visage was perhaps a portent of things to come. (Photo by author)

Bill Devitt at five years of age (left). (Kindergarten picture)

My brother, Bob Devitt (below), age thirteen, in front of our house in St. Paul in July 1944. I was on leave just before going overseas. Note the helmet, carbine, leggings, gas mask, belt and suspenders for a back pack, and the bedroll. In case one should think that the U.S. army was sending thirteen-year olds to Europe to fight its battles, don't worry. The equipment was mine. (Photo by author)

wouldn't believe it. If she ran this boat, we'd have to do it all ourselves."

The officers' meals were served in a dining room with white tablecloths and waiters to serve. The only peculiarity in the food was having boiled potatoes included for breakfast. Perhaps this was standard breakfast fare for Australians, but it wasn't for me.

In contrast to the officers, the enlisted men were issued hammocks. Many of the men couldn't sleep in the hammocks, which would sway back and forth, so they ended up on the deck. They slept in large rooms with perhaps fifty men in each. The same room was used for dining with the food being brought in large containers and served to the men as they filed past with their mess kits.

The mess kit was a rectangular metal pan, about eight inches by six inches and an inch deep, with a folding handle and a removable cover. It was not designed to keep the different foods separated from each other. The servers would place, for example, potatoes with gravy in the mess kit, followed by meat loaf on top, then by green beans, then by canned peaches with juice slopped over the whole thing, and finally a slice of bread with butter and a piece of chocolate cake which would settle down and soak up the grease, gravy, bean juice, and peach juice — an almost unpalatable mess, except to a hungry young man. The mess kit was aptly named.

"I'll Be Seeing You"

One of the lieutenants on the ship was Foster "Bud" Deffenbaugh, from Chicago, who shared a stateroom with me and two others.[1] In real life he had been a musician. Bud got some of us to do a lot of singing, which made the slow journey more agreeable. I remember one song he tried to get me to sing.

---

[1]Bud and I stayed together until we got to the Second Battalion, 330th Infantry Regiment, 83rd Division. At that time, Bud was assigned to battalion Headquarters Company as leader of the A and P (Ammunition and Pioneer) platoon, while I was sent to a rifle company.

I recall it especially since I could never quite get down to the lowest note nor up to the highest. It was a sentimental ballad written for sentimental times entitled "I'll be Seeing You." It went:

> "I'll be seeing you in all the old familiar places
> That this heart of mine embraces
> All day through. In a small café,
> The park across the way,
> The children's carousel,
> The chestnut tree, the wishing well.
> I'll be seeing you in every lovely summer's day,
> In everything that's light and gay.
> I'll always think of you that way.
> I'll find you in the morning sun, and when the night
>   is new,
> I'll be looking at the moon, but I'll be seeing you."*

Today that might sound like sentimental drivel, but to at least one young man on that ship, the song brought out mixed feelings of sadness, fear, and hope. I didn't have a steady girlfriend at home, so I didn't have the feelings of closeness that the song implies. The song filled me with yearning and put me in touch with my unfulfilled longing for sexual intimacy and marriage. I suppose that I subconsciously feared that I might never return home to enjoy such things.

As an unmarried Catholic young man, who, like most of my peers, followed the teaching of the Church in abstaining from sex before marriage, I was saddened at the prospect of never being able to experience the intimate pleasures of married life as well as the joys of a home and children.

---

*Reprinted with permission of the New Irving Kahal Music Company and the Fain Music Company.

Chapter Two

Normandy
August 1944

W E ARRIVED IN LIVERPOOL in early August and marched off the ship and down the street amidst the friendly waves and cheers of the local kids who lined the way. We were trucked inland to a camp where we stayed a few days getting weapons and equipment to go to France. Another truck trip took us south to the English Channel where we sailed out of Southampton to cross the channel to France, about fifty miles away.

The crossing was uneventful and took only a few hours. Although the channel was usually quite rough, I didn't feel even a little seasick. None of the French ports were as yet operating, so we landed at Omaha Beach, the scene of the worst fighting on D-day about two months earlier.

June 6, 1944, was D-Day (the landing day) for the Allied invasion of northern Europe. The Allies had invaded Sicily and Italy in 1943 as part of the strategy to engage the German army with the intention of relieving pressure on the Russians, our allies on the eastern front. They had borne the brunt of the fighting against the Germans from the time the German army had attacked Russia in the summer of 1941. Early in the winter of 1941, the Germans almost succeeded in taking Moscow, and both armies suffered huge losses. The frigid Russian winter together with the determined Russian resistance stopped the German army at the gates of Moscow and forced it to withdraw from its most advanced positions.

The Russians started in early 1942 to press the Allies to open a second front by invading France. Instead of that, the Allies invaded North Africa in the fall of 1942 and Sicily and Italy in the summer of 1943. The Russians were furious at what they considered the small size of the Allied efforts. The Russians were facing hundreds of German divisions, while the Allies were engaging only a dozen or two. The Russians had suffered millions of casualties while the Allied losses were numbered in the tens of thousands.

Joseph Stalin demanded an invasion of France in 1944, and the Allies agreed. The D-Day landings in Normandy finally opened the second front which the Russians had in mind. Although this was a huge operation and probably as large as the Allies could muster, it never did approach the number of troops engaged by the Russians and Germans on the eastern front.

Omaha Beach consisted of a flat sand beach with steep hills and cliffs rising abruptly out of it about a hundred yards from the shore. The Germans had built concrete bunkers overlooking the beach.

After debarking, we immediately walked off the beach along the paths up the hills. Walking to the top of the hill with a full field pack on my back was difficult and tiring, and I remember wondering what it would have been like trying to get up the hill if someone had been shooting at me.

On D-Day, the Germans had machine guns on the part of the beach nearest the hills so that they were able to direct "grazing fire" against the incoming Americans. That is a very important principle of infantry tactics. It is small-arms fire whose trajectory is no higher than a man and therefore never gets far above the ground. The classic use of machine guns defending a level field is to have a machine gun at both ends of the field with the fire from the guns crisscrossing each other. On Omaha Beach, the machine guns were at the rear of the beach near the hills. The machine guns directed grazing fire

Omaha Beach—photo taken by the author in July 1988. This monument was built at the location of a German concrete gun emplacement that brought havoc to the American soldiers on June 6, 1944.

toward the water in such a way that it crisscrossed each other. Anyone advancing toward the hills would have to go through that curtain of death.

Shooting from a hill down toward someone climbing up is called "plunging fire," which is not nearly so effective as grazing fire. Therefore, the most dangerous task on Omaha Beach on D-Day was not advancing up the hill, but was getting through the water and up the beach past the grazing fire.

Soon after landing at Omaha Beach, we were trucked to a bivouac area, an open field surrounded by hedgerows.

I'd never seen nor heard of a hedgerow before. A hedgerow is a row of hedges surrounding a field. Each farmer tills one or more fields within the square of land between the hedges. Over the years the hedgerows grew (some of them were hundreds of years old), and their root systems accumulated soil and debris. The end result is a wall of solid earth four to eight feet in height, topped by bushy hedges or trees.

When the Allied forces landed in Normandy, they were faced with a unique kind of fighting. In order to get from one field to the next, it was often necessary to go over the top of a hedgerow. The Germans would have their machine guns at the opposite end of the field directed to the top of the hedgerow that the attackers would be trying to scale.

Hedgerow fighting was something new to the Americans as it was for the British, Canadians, and other Allies fighting in Normandy. Various tactics were used to overcome the natural defense that the hedgerows gave the Germans.

One tactic was devised by an ingenious American, a Sergeant Culin. He fitted a heavy metal blade looking like a giant scoop shovel on the front of a tank. It would smash into the hedgerow with such force as to break through and allow the infantry who followed to go through and not over the hedgerow. At the same time the attacking force would direct mortar and artillery fire against the Germans to reduce the volume of their fire.

We received a few days' training and orientation in Normandy and then were split up and sent to various units to

A road in Normandy showing hedgerows on either side, June or July 1944. Fortunately for me, I didn't arrive there until about three weeks after the fighting had ended. (Courtesy of the 83rd Infantry Division Association)

replace men killed or wounded in combat. "We" consisted of company-grade officers and enlisted men, privates, corporals, and sergeants, probably between one and two hundred men.

I recall only two things about the training we received. One was that an instructor told us how terror-filled combat would be.

"You men shouldn't be surprised if you get so scared that you pee in your pants," he said. "It might even get so bad that you get a little brown in your shorts."

Fortunately, after I got into combat, I never experienced the underwear problem.

The second was that we were trained thoroughly in hedgerow fighting. But the fighting had advanced out of Normandy and the hedgerow country, so that training went for naught.

Sometime after leaving Omaha Beach, I noticed that all the Jeeps had a vertical metal bar attached to their fronts. The top two or three inches of the bar was bent forward at a forty-five degree angle. I asked a fellow who had landed a few days after D-Day, "What are those bars on the front of the Jeeps?"

"Right after we landed," he replied, "we found out the hard way that the Germans string piano wire across these narrow roads just at the height of the driver. When a Jeep went down the road, the hood would go under the wire, and the wire would get the driver in the neck or head. There were even rumors that some Jeeps ended up with headless drivers. The bar breaks the wire before it gets to the driver."

Those of us who had been indoctrinated in the often unfathomable and illogical world of army rules and regulations might have concluded that the reason for installing the bars was that it was against army regulations to have headless Jeep drivers.

My most vivid recollection of Normandy, other than Omaha Beach and the hedgerows, is having little French children come up to us with their hands out, begging, "Cigarettes pour Papa?" and "Chocolates pour Mama?"

I suspect that the cigarettes and chocolate we gave them did not go entirely to Papa and Mama, but with the wartime scarcity of those items, the young entrepreneurs made a killing on the black market.

Chapter Three

Brittany
August 1944 to September 1944

O N AUGUST 18, 1944, I was assigned to E Company, 330th Infantry Regiment, part of the 83rd Infantry Division. E Company was a rifle company.[2]

When I joined the company, it was in the town of Dinard, and I was assigned by the company commander to be the leader of the third platoon.

The company had just completed about two months of combat, which began in June in Normandy soon after D-Day and ended in capturing Dinard, a lovely resort town on the shore of the Atlantic Ocean where Normandy meets Brittany.

Two other officers joined E Company when I did. One was a first lieutenant, Berry, who was appointed executive officer, second in command of the company. The other was a second lieutenant, Vitulo, whom we called Vit, who was appointed leader of the second platoon. They were both replacements, as I was, for officers who had been killed or wounded in the fighting. None of the three of us had ever been in combat.

The thought of joining a combat unit as a green, untried second lieutenant, a shavetail, with men who had been battle-

---

[2]The table of organization called for a rifle company to have 187 enlisted men and six officers. The rifle company consisted of three rifle platoons, a weapons platoon, and company headquarters. See Appendix B for more detail.

tested in Normandy and Brittany, scares me more now than it did then. I was very much aware of my lack of combat experience and was curious as to how I would behave in combat. Yet despite these feelings of inadequacy, I felt confident in my ability to do my job and lead my men in battle. I don't know what caused me to feel confident. I'm sure that psychologists could give lots of reasons why, such as the color of my socks on my first day in kindergarten or on what side of my head my hair was parted that day. I suppose I thought that if the others could do it, so could I. So, I gritted my teeth and plunged ahead. I wished that I knew more and realized that there were gaps in my knowledge and experience. But to lead well, one must have self-assurance, and if I doubted myself too much, I couldn't lead. So I behaved as I had to, with a sense of confidence, although the confidence was hardly warranted by the facts.

Chambers

The company commander was a first lieutenant, Frank Chambers, who had replaced an earlier company commander. Chambers had won the Silver Star for gallantry in action in Normandy or Brittany. He was a Southerner, from Mississippi, and a proud graduate of Mississippi State University. He was an athlete and had played football and baseball in college. He was not a big man, probably five-foot-ten and about 170 pounds, with a pleasant sense of humor. The bridge of his nose was rather flat, the result of an old football injury. His eyes seemed to be squinting constantly, like those of a tiger, although, unlike the tiger's, his eyes exuded a feeling of mirth, not menace. He did his job well without bearing down unduly or trying to be tough on his subordinates. He liked to reminisce about his college days. I still remember his talking about "Bruiser" Kinard, a great football player (a tackle) from Mississippi. He'd say, "Ya'll probably don't remember Bruiser Kinard. There wasn't anyone like him, not Red Grange or Bronko Nagurski. If he'd been a running back and from the north he'd've been the most famous player in the country. When he hit the line of scrimmage, those opposing linemen would fly in all directions like they were hit by a ten-ton truck."

One of the first things I noticed about Chambers was that he wore a shiny bright blue raincoat. The American Army raincoat, which the rest of us wore, was a dull, drab green quite unlike Chambers' snappy number. He got his from a German prisoner, probably an officer judging from the quality of the material. He wore it proudly even though it hung down almost to his heels so that he looked like a pyramidal tent moving along with a helmeted head sticking out the top.

Sandler

The leader of the first platoon was a first lieutenant, David Sandler, who had been in combat and had returned from the hospital at about the time I joined the company. He still had some unhealed shrapnel wounds on his back, which needed new bandages every few days. Sandler was Jewish. He was older than the rest of us, probably about thirty. His hair was reddish brown, thinning a little on top. Physically he was possibly the best specimen in the company, being about six feet tall with broad shoulders and a muscular build. He originally came from one of the Baltic countries—Lithuania, I believe. Although he spoke English well, it was with a slight accent. He had no love for the Russians who had taken over his country, nor for the Germans, who were our enemies and were brutally maltreating the Jews.

He was a good-sized fellow with a real appetite. I remember his finishing a big meal and remarking that he could use a little more food and going over to the mess sergeant in the chow line with his mess kit in hand and saying, "Sergeant, do you have a few more potatoes? They were really good. Thanks. Just toss a little gravy on them. If you have a couple more pieces of bread, that goes good with gravy. And some more of those baked beans will help out. Thanks a lot. And how about a touch more coffee? I see you've got some cake left over. Why don't you throw a piece on top?".

Frank Chambers (above) in front of a slightly damaged building in Brittany, August 1944. (Photo courtesy of Shirley Johnson, daughter of Frank Chambers)

Frank Chambers and David Sandler (right), the two most experienced officers in E Company when I joined them. Fall of 1944. (Courtesy of Shirley Johnson)

Sandler left the hospital before he was entirely healed so that he could continue to fight Germans. To return to a combat unit voluntarily, before one's hospital stay was completed, was otherwise unheard of in my experience. Returning to combat as an infantryman meant almost certain death or injury. No wonder that infantrymen were not anxious to rejoin their units. There weren't any medals given for returning voluntarily to one's company, as Sandler did, but there should have been.

Bonnet

Walter Bonnet was leader of the third platoon when I arrived. He was from Iowa or western Illinois and about twenty-five years old. His speech was rather slow, and since he was from my part of the country, he was blessed with not having an accent, something with which (I believed at the time) everyone from almost every other part of the country was burdened. He was a technical sergeant (See Appendix B) who had been platoon sergeant, second in command. He later became platoon leader when the lieutenant he replaced was killed or wounded. When I arrived, Bonnet reverted back to platoon sergeant. He had been in E Company in the States, and had fought all through Normandy and Brittany. He had much more army experience than I and also had combat experience, something which must be lived and can't be taught. I wonder now what he thought when he had to give up command of the platoon to a fellow who was younger, less experienced, and totally new to combat. We never talked about it. But he recognized, as I did, that the army system was to replace fallen men with men of similar rank. If he ever resented my presence, I was not aware of it.

When I first met Bonnet, he had two holes in his helmet. When he was the platoon leader in Normandy, the men would not go over the top of a hedgerow for fear of the German small arms fire. "Come on, you guys," he said. "If we don't get over

The officers of E Company (above), 330th Infantry, fall of 1944. Left to right: Lieutenants Vitulo, Sandler, Devitt, Chambers, Packer, and Berry. (Courtesy of Shirley Johnson) Walter Bonnet (lower left) outside a German dugout in which we lived near Dinard in Brittany in the fall of 1944. (Photo by the author) The NCOs of the third platoon of E Company (lower right), fall of 1944. Left to right, front: Walter Bonnet, unknown, Michael Hluska; standing: George Danniello, Enos Ramsey, Talmer Brill, and Warren Martinson. The shadow taking the picture was myself. (Photo by author)

this thing, we'll never get out of here. It's let up some. Look, it's not so bad now. What are ya afraid of?"

He then cautiously started to look over the top of the hedgerow. As his head appeared, a German bullet struck the helmet, pierced it, and came out a few inches from where it had entered. Bonnet was not touched. The explanation is that inside the steel helmet was a fiber helmet liner that rested on his head, so there was a slight distance between his head and the helmet. The German bullet traveled the fraction of an inch between the inside of the steel helmet and Bonnet's head.

I don't know what his men's reaction to this was, but I'd guess they were even more reluctant to go over the top after the near miss.

Bread and Jam

When one is away from home, eating becomes a high priority late in the evening when there is no kitchen or ice box to offer the possibility of a snack. A few days after I joined E Company, a couple of sergeants in my platoon asked me to get some food out of the mess tent. This was after dark and long after dinner, so we were all hungry. One of them said to me, "Lieutenant, could you use some bread and jam? I sure could. The mess sergeant knows the two of us so well that if he only saw us from the back, he'd know us. So we thought that you could take your flashlight and go in and get us a loaf of bread and a can of that strawberry jam. How about it?"

"Well, Sergeant, I don't know if I should, " I said.

"Oh, Lieutenant, we do it all the time. Boy, it's a long time to breakfast."

After thinking a moment, which was not long enough, I said, "Okay, I'll do it."

Why didn't the sergeants get the food themselves? I suppose they thought that rather than run the risk of being caught, it would be safer to have the new, young, inexperienced lieutenant do the job. The mess sergeant and cooks slept in a tent nearby. I didn't think at the time what would happen if I were discovered taking food out of the mess tent. If a private were caught, he would probably have been punished. But what would happen if one of the people whose job it was to see that the food was fairly distributed was found with his hand in the cookie jar? In retrospect, I surely should not have done it. Nevertheless, when the mess sergeant and cooks seemed to have gone to sleep, I went quietly into the mess tent with a flashlight. I soon found a loaf of bread and a can of jam. As I was walking out, I heard the mess sergeant's voice, "Is someone in there?" I didn't reply but quickly walked away and out of sight. Despite the close call with the mess sergeant, the other sergeants and I enjoyed the bread and jam.

A day or two later, I returned from a meeting to the platoon area after dark. The men were sitting around a campfire (we were not in a combat zone), and someone said, "Come on, Lieutenant, have a piece of bread before it's all gone. There's still some of that great strawberry jam in the can. Here's a spoon to dig it out with."

The only light was from the campfire, so it was impossible to see into the can which I had so recently purloined. After I spooned a liberal portion of jam onto the bread, I took a big bite. I immediately let out a yell. At the same time everyone near me started to roll on the ground with laughter. Bees had got into the can, and several were in my mouth. The men had waited patiently for me to take a bite of bread and jam, and I did not disappoint them.

Although I must have gotten several bees in my mouth, I spat them out without being stung. Perhaps the good Lord was teaching me a lesson.

Liquor Ration

Sometime after joining E Company, I was informed that the officer's liquor ration was coming. Every few weeks each officer was allowed to purchase two or three bottles of liquor. I had heard in the movies about the rum ration the British navy dispensed to its sailors in the days of Captain Bligh of "Mutiny on the Bounty" fame, but I had never heard, nor could scarcely believe, that a liquor ration existed in the American army. At least the British had the good grace and common sense to issue the rum ration to all ranks, whereas the American liquor ration went only to the officers.

I don't know how this was expected to be handled. Perhaps each officer was supposed to duck behind a tree and take a couple of belts from the bottle and then emerge, smiling, to instruct his men on the evils of alcohol.

I was barely twenty-one years old and had very limited experience with alcohol. We had a choice of the type of liquor, gin, rum, bourbon, or whatever else was available. Since I didn't know gin from gin rummy, I called upon Bonnet for help. I said to him, "Bonnet, I really don't drink. Why don't you take this stuff and give it out to whoever wants it. Don't be afraid to save a sip or two for yourself."

He smiled and said, "Thanks, Lieutenant. I might even stretch it to three sips. Don't worry. I'll take care of it. This'll taste good after that cheap wine in Normandy. Sure you don't want some?"

"No, just keep it. Just be sure no one drinks too much."

"Don't worry, Lieutenant. With only two bottles for the whole platoon, no one'll get too much. The men'll appreciate it."

This system seemed to work well, for I never heard a complaint from anyone.

Ile de Cezembre

Before we left Dinard, E Company had one further task. Although the city of Dinard had been taken from the Germans, they continued to hold an island, Ile de Cezembre, in Dinard Bay, and this prevented the Americans from using the port. In August 1944, there were no ports open for supplying the Allied forces, so the landing beaches in Normandy were still being used. Therefore, it was vital that the Ile de Cezembre be taken from the Germans so that the ports of Dinard and Saint Malo, which adjoined Dinard, could be opened. The Second Battalion of the 330th Infantry, which included E Company, was ordered to assault the island.

The island was about 1,000 yards from shore and stood out of the water like the top of a hill. It was fairly round in shape and was probably 500 feet across. The Germans had fortified it very heavily. There were big guns dug into the rocks, and tunnels and living quarters were burrowed deep into the ground, making it difficult to knock them out.

A few days after I joined E Company, we started preparations for attacking the island. The company was assigned an area of the beach to assault, and my platoon was assigned a portion of it. We spent the next week practicing landing from assault boats. Each platoon would get into an assault boat and go out into a part of the bay that was out of sight from Ile de Cezembre. We would circle around in the water for a while and then land on a designated beach similar to the island's beach.

While we were in the water, we weren't allowed to stand up and look over the sides. I'd say, "Men, keep your heads down. We can't look over the sides. If they were firing at us, you'd keep your heads down for sure. We're trying to get used to keeping our heads down so when we approach the island, some of us won't stick our heads up out of curiosity and have them shot off."

The main reason we wanted to put our heads up was to get fresh air to overcome the sea-sickness from the rocking of the boat. At first everyone would keep his head down and then after a while someone would throw up on the deck. This seemed to open the flood gates and more and more would throw up wherever they could. Some would put their heads over the sides and soon everyone would be standing up to get fresh air. I was one of them, so there was no use trying to enforce an order I couldn't follow myself.

At the same time we were practicing landings, another method was tried to make the Germans surrender the island. Each day it was bombed by B-24 Liberator bombers and P-38 Lightning fighters. The B-24 was a large, four-engine bomber that was bombing Germany in great numbers almost daily. The island was so small that the B-24s had to fly over it one at a time to drop their bombs. They couldn't fly in V shaped formations as they normally did, for if they did, most of the bombs would have landed in the water. The P-38s bombed and strafed the island, and our artillery also shelled it regularly. At the end of each day, we would check with headquarters to see if the Germans had surrendered. The answer was always, "No."

After a week of bombing, shelling, and practicing landings, we were ordered to assault the island the next day.

The next morning at about 6:00 A.M., we got up and prepared to go down to the beach to carry out the assault. I hadn't been in combat before, so I had a rather morbid curiosity as to how, and how many, of our men would die. I also had a recurring worry as to how well I would do my job. Charging up a heavily defended beach was sure to cause us many casualties, but we didn't talk about it. Since I had not been in combat and many of my men had, I was concerned that I would be brave enough and have my wits about me sufficiently to lead my men as well as they deserved to be led. I'm sure that I had an underlying fear of being a coward in the face of enemy fire. But I don't know of any way of predicting how any single person would react during his first experience with combat.

Just before we were to climb on the trucks to go down to the water to board the assault boats, Chambers, the company commander, called the company together. He got up on the hood of a jeep and said, "Men, I've got good news. Colonel Norris just called and told me that the Germans on the island surrendered a half hour ago. We'll take the rest of the day off. Whoever wants to go into town can get a pass from the first sergeant. Remember the war isn't over yet, so don't celebrate too much."

The heavy aerial bombing and the artillery shelling had succeeded. There was little cheering or yelling or other celebrating. I remember feeling very relieved at narrowly avoiding a slaughter, which might have been a miniature D-Day, with our men dying on the beach and drowning in the water.

Ile de Cezembre, Dinard, France, July 1988. Was this island worth dying for? I don't know, but the men of E Company, 330th Infantry were prepared to die to retake it in August 1944. (Photo by author) The A & P (Ammunition and Pioneer) Platoon (below) of the Second Battalion, 330th Infantry Regiment in Dinard. In the lower left corner is Lieutenant Foster "Bud" Deffenbaugh, leader of the platoon (with sunglasses and the lieutenant bar on his shirt collar). This photo was taken the morning we were to attack the Germans on the Ile de Cezembre in late August 1944. (Photo courtesy of 83rd Infantry Division Association)

Chapter Four

Luxembourg
September 1944 to November 1944

I N EARLY SEPTEMBER, WE got into trucks and traveled to the Grand Duchy of Luxembourg, a tiny country wedged between France, Germany, and Belgium. The American forces that had preceded us had just driven the Germans out of Luxembourg, so when we arrived there, riding in trucks, the people of Luxembourg lined the roads and cheered us as liberators, even though we had not fired a shot in their country. Since I had not yet been in combat, I felt a little like an imposter while smiling and waving to the cheers of the crowds. I'm sure that those who had been in combat had no such feelings.

Many of the people were waving little American flags. I couldn't figure out where the people in the small towns we went through had found American flags. Maybe with Europe's history of frequent wars, the people always were prepared by having a few flags of any potential friend or foe on hand to wave for whichever army arrived on the scene.

Bed Check Charlie

Since Luxembourg was a combat area, we were careful not to have fires at night. In a non-combat area we would usually sit around a campfire at night when we were living outdoors. But in the combat areas, the Germans would often send an airplane over the battle lines in the evening to discover the

Moselle River (July 1988), showing Germany in the background and Luxembourg on the near side of the river. Note the vineyard in the foreground, from which the renown Moselle wines are made. In 1944 we were there later in the season so that the grape leaves were so thick that we could hide behind them and observe the Germans on the other side. (Photo by the author)

location of the American positions. We called these spotter
planes Bed Check Charlie. When we heard Bed Check Charlie
coming, we made doubly sure that there were no lights or fires,
including cigarettes, visible from the air.

Our mission in Luxembourg was twofold: first, to train
in preparation for attacking into Germany, and second, to
maintain a defensive position along the Moselle River, which
separated Luxembourg from Germany. The Germans were on
the east side of the river, and we were on the west.

While other units took up defensive positions on the
Moselle, E Company began its stay in Luxembourg by con-
ducting training exercises.

On some days, Chambers, the company commander,
would send each of the three rifle platoons into the field for
training. Each platoon would, for example, practice attacking
a fortified hill. The platoon leader would explain to his men the
hypothetical situation. He might have said that the hill was
held by a German patrol. The platoon leader would then give
an order directing the way the simulated attack was to be exe-
cuted. He might have had two squads attack from the front
and the third squad attack from the side. Each squad leader
would give orders to his men as how to attack up the hill. While
some men would pretend to be firing, others would run forward
a few yards and then fall to the ground and pretend to be firing while the others would be running forward. The maneuver
is called "Fire and Movement," and is a basic method of infantry attack. Once the platoon captured the hill, we would sit
down and critique the exercise.

The Division Exercise

Usually we didn't have live ammunition, nor would supporting weapons such as mortars or machine guns be used.
On one occasion, however, we had a platoon exercise that was
supervised by several officers from division headquarters. The
group included a lieutenant colonel or a major, together with
two or three captains and lieutenants thrown in to add ballast.

The third platoon was to attack a hill. It was devoid of trees and gullies that would provide cover and concealment for an attacking force. The distance from our line of departure (the place from which we commenced the attack) to the top of the hill was about 300 yards.

As part of our support, eighty-one-millimeter mortars, manned by personnel from H Company, were to be fired over our heads using white phosphorous shells. They would provide a smoke screen between us and the top of the hill where the imagined enemy was located.

Before the attack, I called together the three squad leaders, the platoon sergeant, and the platoon guide. We met in a little clump of trees and bushes about 500 yards from the top of the hill which was our objective. I gave them my order: "We're to take that hill. We think there are fifteen to twenty-five Krauts defending it. The first and second squads will attack from the front. The third squad will advance to the left flank of the hill and lay down a base of fire while the other two squads attack up the hill. H Company will fire white phosphorus in front of the first and second squads to conceal their approach. The line of departure is the bottom of the hill. All three squads will cross the line of departure at 10:00 A.M. I'll be with the first and second squads, the platoon sergeant will be with the third, and the platoon guide will stay in the rear. Watch for my signal to commence the attack. Let's synchronize our watches. I have 9:48. You've got about ten minutes to brief your men. Any questions? No questions? Move out."

As the platoon moved up the hill, several rounds of white phosphorus landed, as planned, one or two hundred yards ahead of us. As we continued our advance, however, a shell landed unexpectedly among us. (This is called a short round, since it fell short of its target.) It landed about fifty yards to my left front and within a few yards of several of the men. When a white phosphorous round explodes, it spews burning phosphorous in all directions, forming a cloud of smoke. When the short round landed someone yelled, "Let's get the hell out of here!"

Immediately the men near the exploded shell ran, thinking that more short rounds might land among them.

No one was burned by the shell, though, and no other rounds landed short. But our attack was disrupted. After some delay, we advanced to the top of the hill and completed the exercise.

The division headquarters officers criticized the platoon severely for running when the white phosphorous landed. One of them said, "You men have got to realize you can't run whenever a shell lands near you in combat. For one thing, you'd be running all the time. For another, that's just what the Germans want, to get you out of your positions. Besides, if you get up and run, you're more likely to be hit than if you stay put on the ground."

That was true. But we weren't in combat. Why should the men have stayed where they were and risked other shells landing short and killing them in a training exercise? While the people in division headquarters told us to risk our lives in training, they did not risk theirs in training and probably not even in combat. Officers in division headquarters did not experience combat the way men in a rifle company did. A soldier in a rifle company would go days or even weeks with his life constantly at risk. A shell fragment or a bullet could hit him at any time. An officer in division headquarters might be at the front occasionally, but he didn't run nearly the risk that the front-line soldier did. It still makes me angry when I think that our men were demeaned and criticized by officers who probably knew less about combat than many of them and who were certainly not putting their lives on the line the way we were soon to do.

Martinson

The other incident arising out of the division exercise had to do with Warren Martinson. Marty was a pretty big man, probably six feet and about 200 pounds. Unlike most of the other men, he didn't have the hardened appearance of one who was in good shape. He had a round face and didn't appear very muscular, especially around the middle. He was a fellow Minnesotan whom I had appointed leader of one of the platoon's three squads. Marty didn't want to be a squad leader.

A few weeks earlier, I'd said to him, "Marty, I want you to be leader of the second squad. I've talked it over with Sergeant Bonnet, and we think you're the man for the job."

"Lieutenant," he said, "I'm just a country boy from Minnesota. I've never had any training to be a squad leader. I'm just not cut out for it."

"Marty," I said, "I'm just a city boy from Minnesota, and I don't know much about what I'm doing. But we're both stuck here. You'll do fine. I want you to take the job."

Marty smiled and said, "Okay, Lieutenant, if you say so."

Marty was a private first class, so I sent in a request that he be appointed sergeant, the prescribed rank of a squad leader.

At the critique, the division officers criticized the platoon not only for running from the white phosphorous but also for the performance of the members of the platoon in failing to use proper arm and hand signals. "What's the signal for enemy in sight?" one of the division officers asked Marty.

Marty looked at him and hesitated for a few seconds and then shook his head and said, "I don't know, sir. I just don't remember."

He was obliged to confess this in front of the whole platoon, including, of course, the members of his own squad.

The embarrassment was too much for Marty. As soon as we got back to the company bivouac area, he told me he would no longer be a squad leader. He said, "Lieutenant, I just don't want to be a squad leader. I'm just no good at it. You can see what those officers from division thought of me. You've gotta get someone else."

"Marty, you'll probably never use that signal in combat. Why I didn't remember it myself," I lied.

"Lieutenant, I told you before that I didn't have what it takes. I can't do it."

"Marty, you've done a good job. The men all like you. I want you to stay on."

"Lieutenant, I can't. They made me look like an asshole in front of the whole platoon. That's too much. You've gotta get someone else."

So I replaced Marty, and he reverted back to rifleman.

The Marty incident angered me more than anything else in the division exercise. To criticize a leader in front of his men was, in my estimation, a cardinal sin in dealing with soldiers. As a result, we lost the use of a man in an important job—one that was not easy to fill.

I wonder if the division officers realized the damage they did to our platoon. I think not. The critiquers should have been critiqued and told that they were not playing games, but were dealing with people's lives.

The Mysterious Noise

During part of our time in Luxembourg, the platoon was stationed in a large house we called "the Chateau." It was about a quarter of a mile from the west bank of the Moselle River. The Germans were on the east side of the river, across from us. The Chateau lay in a valley behind the river's high west bank. One squad would be dug in near the top of the hill overlooking the river in order to observe any movement by the Germans and to defend against attack. The river banks were covered by long rows of grape vines, which grew on tall sticks. The men would conceal themselves among the large grape leaves while observing the Germans across the river. The other two squads stayed in reserve at the Chateau.

One day we received orders to send a patrol each night down to a little town on our side of the river to be sure that the Germans were not there. We were to send patrols into the town, from which the townspeople had been evacuated, every night for a week or two.

Before sending out the first patrol, I decided that the patrol would be a squad—twelve men. I also decided that I

"The Chateau" in 1944 (top). I don't know where the child in the front door came from. I thought all the civilians had been evacuated. The same "Chateau" in 1988 (bottom) with the current owner and my wife, Mary, who didn't want to be photographed because she said she was too heavy. I couldn't wait for her to lose ten pounds. (Photos by author)

would lead the patrol for the first three nights, with a different squad going out each night.

The reason for leading the first three was to show each squad how I wanted the patrol to be conducted. Besides, I thought it well for morale purposes to let the men know that I was willing to take the personal risks involved in patrolling.

After the first three nights each squad leader would, in turn, lead his own squad on patrol.

The plan was to leave after dark and follow a twisting roadway to the town on the river bank. After we arrived, we were to observe for a few minutes, then return by the same route. Our orders were to take no more than three hours.

On the first patrol, we left the Chateau as soon as the night reached pitch black. There were no lights anywhere. The windows in the Chateau were blacked out, and the town was dark, since nobody was in it. I don't recall whether there was any moonlight, but I do remember that the night was very dark and quiet.

The patrol walked in two columns single file on either side of the road, and I, as the leader, led one of the columns. We started out walking very slowly and cautiously, with the men following each other, not far apart. I was concerned about walking into a town that might be occupied by German soldiers lying in ambush for us. Before we started out, I said, "Be sure to pick up your feet when you walk and step as quietly as possible. If there are any Krauts out there, they've got nothing to do but listen for us. We don't want to sound like a bunch of jitterbugs[3] dancing out there on the road. So keep quiet."

About every twenty-five yards, I would halt the patrol, with a hand signal, to look and listen. After we had proceeded about 200 yards from the Chateau we heard a loud thump off to one side of the road. I halted the men and looked in the direction of the noise. After a few minutes, and hearing or seeing nothing further, we continued down the road. Soon we

---

[3]The jitterbug was a strenuous dance performed to quick-tempo jazz or swing music.

heard a thump and then another. We all hit the ground and pointed our weapons in the direction of the noise. I sent two men to see what it was. The rest of us remained quiet while the two proceeded into the dark. We lay there like hunters waiting expectantly in a forest for a trophy deer to appear through the underbrush. While the two were gone we heard further thumps —which didn't reduce our anxiety. After five or ten minutes (which seemed like an hour), the two men returned. I whispered to them, "What's that noise?"

"Oh," one of them replied, "It's just apples falling from the trees."

It was fall—and there was nobody around to pick the apples.

On the night of the apple incident, we did not even get to the town. I set such a slow pace that after about two hours we had not reached the town. I had the patrol turn around and return to the Chateau so we would be back within the three-hour-time limit. Although we patrolled for several more nights, the apple incident was the most memorable event on any of the patrols.

Colonel Robert Foster was commander of the 330th Infantry Regiment. He was about fifty years of age, with black hair and a narrow mustache. He was a United States Military Academy graduate, a West Pointer. I don't know if this was a reason that he was very strict and serious. When we wore summer clothing, Colonel Foster always wore freshly starched pants and shirt, while the rest of us were not so tidy.

Lieutenant Colonel John Norris was the commander of the Second Battalion of the 330th Infantry. He was also a West Pointer, a tall, lanky man who was probably in his late twenties. In contrast to Colonel Foster, he graced us with a ready smile and a pleasant demeanor. I still remember an expression he used when talking about the men in his command. He would use the term "your people" instead of "your men."

The Inspection

Sometime after the apple incident, I received a telephone call from battalion headquarters advising me that Colonel Foster was on his way, with Colonel Norris, to inspect our area and warning me to be ready for the brass. Facing Colonel Foster was a very tense prospect, but I knew Colonel Norris better and felt that he was more sympathetic to the problems of second lieutenants.

We had about ten minutes before they were to arrive. I tried to anticipate what Colonel Foster would be looking for in an inspection. I thought that he would come into the Chateau and in the military tradition look for specks of dust in the most outlandish places possible such as on the tops of doors and unreachable corners of the closets. If we couldn't outlast the Germans on the battlefield, we might at least defeat them in a housekeeping contest.

The first thing I thought of was to have the Chateau clean and neat; therefore I told the men to sweep the steps and floors throughout the entire building. Then I posted a guard at the front door. One squad was up on the hill overlooking the river, and the other two squads were at the Chateau. I wanted those two squads to appear busy when the colonels arrived, so after the sweeping was finished I had the men cleaning their weapons or doing something else that would appear useful to the colonels.

When they arrived, Colonel Foster didn't even walk into the building. In order to get there they had to take a narrow road through a valley that was heavily wooded with thick underbrush.

I met the two colonels at the front of the building and reported to Colonel Foster, giving my name and rank. The first thing he asked was where our outposts were in the valley. Since this was a combat area, the colonel assumed we would have guards (outposts) located near the road in case a German patrol should come along. At night we did have outposts stationed there, but I didn't think it necessary to have them during the day.

Instead of explaining candidly to Colonel Foster why we had outposts only at night, I tried to bluff him by saying that an outpost was in the bushes. Colonel Foster would not be fooled. "Where are your outposts, Lieutenant?" he asked.

"Well, sir, we've got one outpost hidden back there in the bushes. You must have passed him on the way here."

"No. I didn't see anyone. You show me just where he is."

Of course I couldn't show him, since nobody was out there. It was clear to both colonels that I had lied to Colonel Foster. This, certainly, was embarrassing to Colonel Norris. As they left, he said to me over his shoulder, "I'll talk to you later."

Probably I was the least forthright lieutenant in Colonel Foster's command, but possibly I was not the most stupid. After I'd finished my lying session with him, he asked me, perhaps curious as to whether I knew anything at all, "Lieutenant, how do you describe the security you should have for this situation?"

Fortunately I was able to remember the correct answer. "All around security, sir," I replied.[4]

This bit of quick recall likely saved me from Colonel Foster's dealing with me more harshly.

I still wish that I'd stood up to Colonel Foster and told him truthfully that we didn't need outposts during the day but that we had them in place at night. Why did I lie to him? I don't know. Without time to think I had to give a quick answer, and I suspect that I surmised that the colonel would accept my statement that there was an outpost hidden in the bushes. To this day I still flail myself mentally for being so wrong.

Although this incident worried me much (I thought that Colonel Norris might have replaced me), I heard nothing more about it.

---

[4]All around security is the principle that states: when in a defensive position, the outposts (security) should not only be to the front, facing the enemy, but all around the held position in the event the enemy might approach from the rear or the side.

Since there was never a barbershop available to us, we had to find a way to get a haircut. We had a man, Enos Ramsey, in the third platoon, who had a scissors, a clipper, and a comb, and he cut hair. I don't know how he happened to have this equipment. He was from rural western Virginia, and store-bought haircuts were probably not in vogue there, so he might have thought it best to bring his barbering equipment with him. We didn't worry about hair styling, especially since Ramsey cut hair in only one style-short. He had a tremor in his hands, so submitting to him with a scissors in his trembling hands added excitement to the barbering experience. We'd sit outside on a box, and Ramsey would not ask how we wanted our hair cut, but rather would immediately start cutting in the only way he knew, fast and short. When he finished we'd give him a few francs as pay, thankful that we didn't lose an ear.

"Calling" Artillery

After a few weeks at the Chateau the platoon was moved to a town on the Moselle. It was in this town that I first heard enemy artillery fire. I'm surprised that I don't recall the exact time and place that I first heard that sound.

On a few occasions, the Germans fired artillery at us but nothing fell close enough to cause any casualties. More frequently, the Americans would fire artillery at the Germans. We had 105-millimeter howitzers. Whenever we noticed movement or activity on the German side we would call for fire from our artillery, which was located a few thousand yards behind our position. Our artillery would have a forward observer to direct the fire. He would be on the front lines with us. He might have been called the artillery's infantryman, or the infantry's artilleryman.

When he saw a German target, the forward observer would radio or telephone back to the men at the guns and tell them its location. The artillery would then fire a round. If that first round landed, say, 300 feet over the target, the forward observer would tell the men at the guns to fire a round "down 400 feet." When the second round landed, presumably about

100 feet short of the target, the target would be "bracketed." After that, the forward observer would call back "Up 100 feet. Fire for effect." The artillery would then fire four or more rounds at the target.

In order to call the artillery with accuracy, the forward observer had to know the location of our guns. He had to be able to ascertain the line gun-target. This was an imaginary line running from the gun to the target. If the guns were directly behind the observer, then the observer would be in the line gun-target. This was the best location from the observer's viewpoint, since he could call the location of the round when it landed exactly as it appeared to be from where he was. But, if the guns were not directly behind him, then the line gun-target would not be the same as the line observer-target. If the guns were not directly behind the observer, a round that appeared (from the observer's position) to be 300 feet over the target, would (from the gun's position) be, say, 250 feet over and 100 feet left. So the observer would have to make the adjustment.

One day we noticed some German soldiers moving into a wooded area across the river. There were ten to fifteen of them, and they were only a mile from us. If we could have gotten artillery fire into the area quickly and accurately, we could have disrupted the Germans' operations. Unfortunately, the forward observer was not available. For some reason, he was not in the town with us at the time. Since immediate action was important, I decided to call the artillery myself. The forward observers had binoculars and probably an instrument to help them to judge distances. I had nothing but my four eyes— two plus two eye glasses.

The first round was 400 feet short, so I called the artillery to fire the next round up 500 feet. I said something like, "That's 400 short. So up 500." But the next round, instead of being up 500, was up 450 and left 100. I called for two or three more rounds, and each round was off the target. Obviously something was wrong. The fellow at the guns to whom I was giving the directions said to me, "You don't know what the hell you're doing. Get someone who does."

"Listen," I said, "I don't know what's wrong, but if you can do better, let's trade places. You come up here, and I'll go back where you are and play garrison soldier and sleep in a bed. By the way, just where are you?"

"We're in the bend in the river just south of you," he answered.

Immediately a light went on in my head. I had thought that the guns were to my rear, but instead they were almost directly to my right. The bend in the river was south of me, to my right, and the guns were in that bend. I failed to determine the line gun-target and made a mess of the operation. Needless to say, whenever I called artillery in the future, I found out, before firing, the location of the guns. And I promised myself never again to challenge the man at the guns.

Dinner with the Mayor

Another interesting, but less traumatic, incident took place in a small town in which my platoon was billeted for a few weeks. One Sunday I was invited to dinner at the home of the town's mayor. I was told that I should bring a translator who spoke French, so I brought the only fellow in the platoon who did. His first name was John. He came from northern Maine and was of French descent.

John and I arrived at the mayor's home and, after introductions, sat down at the dining room table. It became clear immediately why I needed an interpreter. I spoke only English, and the mayor only Luxembourgese. Therefore, for me to converse with him, I had to speak to John in English. John spoke to the mayor's wife in French, and she talked to the mayor in Luxembourgese. It went something like this:

Devitt to the Mayor (in English), "Please pass the butter."

John to the Mayor's wife (in French), "Please pass the butter."

Mayor's wife to the Mayor (in Luxembourgese), "Please pass the butter."

Devitt to the Mayor (in English), "Thank you."

John to the Mayor's wife (in French), "Thank you."

Mayor's wife to the Mayor (in Luxembourgese), "Thank you."

Mayor to Devitt (in Luxembourgese), "You're welcome."

Mayor's wife to John (in French), "You're welcome.

John to Devitt (in English), "You're welcome."

With such an arrangement, very little small talk was exchanged between the mayor and me. Obviously it would have taken only a half dozen or so "Please pass the butters" to have kept us talking all evening.

I'd like to go into more detail as to what was said and what we had to eat. I'd like to, but I just don't remember. It would be pleasant to recall that we started out with a glass or two of Dry Sak, followed by oysters on the half shell, and a small bowl of vichyssoise. This might have been followed by a main course of escargot, truffles, roast goose, and the trimmings. During the meal we might have quaffed a goodly amount of Estate Rothschild wine. After dinner, Napoleon brandy might have been enjoyed from Baccarat crystal brandy snifters.

All of this would have been nice to recall—if it had been true. But somehow such a meal would have been a bit incongruous in an out-of-the-way country village in which the piles of steamy animal manure were heaped next to the houses, since the barns were attached to them, and in which we had to be careful to scrape the manure from our shoes before entering the house.

Sweaters

As the weather got colder, we began to get winter clothing. One of the first items was woolen sweaters. When the company received its sweaters, there were not enough for everyone. The supply sergeant, rather than waiting to receive a second issuance enough for the entire company, distributed what he first received. From that first distribution each platoon got only three sweaters. I suspect that every man in company headquarters, but surely all of the supply sergeant's men, didn't have to wait for the second delivery.

When the first three sweaters arrived, I wish I'd said to the three squad leaders, "Each of you take a sweater and give it to one of the men in your squad. When the rest of the sweaters come in, give them out, but you be the last to get one."

An officer's first concern should be for his men. That is a basic doctrine of leadership. So who got the three sweaters? I don't recall specifically, but I believe that Lieutenant William Devitt was one of the lucky three. Although everyone else received sweaters shortly after the first delivery, this incident was probably the low light in my career as far as to seeing that my men came first.

Somewhere in Normandy the company captured an old German panel truck that we used to carry supplies and equipment. Since we couldn't have campfires after dark when we were behind the front lines, the evenings became long and tedious. The officers in the company had a solution to this. After dark, all six of us would climb into the back of the truck, put a blanket over the rear window, light our kerosene lantern and play poker. We would sit on the floor with our knees tucked under our chins to allow us to squeeze into the limited space like passengers on a packed city bus during rush hour. After two or three hours of sitting in such an uncomfortable position, we would get out of the truck, sometimes after midnight, and be so stiff that we had trouble straightening up and walking.

One evening Chambers, who was the dealer and was the big winner that night, stopped shuffling the cards and said with a wide grin, "Did I ever tell ya'll about the time I hit a double in the last of the ninth to beat 'Ol' Miss' for the conference championship?"

"No," said Berry, who was a little ahead at the time. "Let's hear about it."

A panel truck that E Company liberated from the Germans, fall of 1944. The officers would often play poker in it well into the night. (Photo by author)

Vitulo, who was no shrinking violet and was about even, said to his commanding officer, "Oh sure, go ahead. I've only heard the story a dozen times before."

Sandler, Packer, and Devitt, the big losers, looked at each other and then said in unison, "Deal the cards."

Combat Fatigue

During the month of October, we heard rumors that we were going to be part of a huge attack by the Third Army (Patton's Third Army) in an effort to break through the German defenses and bring the war to an end. It rained frequently, so the attack kept being postponed. The wet weather would have caused the tanks to get mired in the mud. We all looked with anticipation, and some fear, to the proposed operation.

One of the men in the platoon—I'll call him Jones— seemed especially concerned about what might happen. He had been through the Normandy campaign and, I think, wounded there. Since Normandy was the lengthiest and severest battle in which our division had taken part, he probably had suffered through more combat than most of the men in the company. He had also heard some news from home that had disturbed him.

One of the duties of the junior officers was to censor the outgoing mail. That meant that I had to read all the mail written by the men in my platoon to be sure that no important military information was contained in it. Soon after Jones received the disturbing news from home, he came to me with a letter he wanted to mail. He said, "Lieutenant, this letter's very personal. I don't want to talk about it, but would you do me a favor?"

"Sure, Jones, what is it?" I said.

"Well, you see . . . uh . . . well, you see . . . uh, I don't want anyone to read the letter. Would you mind not reading it? There's stuff in there that's private."

"Don't worry, Jones, I'm glad to help. Lick the envelope and give it here."

Jones licked and sealed the envelope and handed it to me. I then signed as censor and put it with the other outgoing mail. I later learned from Bonnet that the letter was about an affair of the heart.

One evening several men, including Jones, got hold of some wine, and possibly something stronger, and they did some drinking. I was not present. About midnight I was awakened and told to go over to Jones' tent. I hurried to his tent and saw him on the ground, thrashing around, with foam coming from his mouth, and crying out in a foreign language.

I grabbed him by the shoulders and said, "Come on, Jones, snap out of it. What's wrong? Take it easy."

I shook him, but he didn't even open his eyes. He kept trying to roll around, and foam came out of his mouth as he babbled on in some incomprehensible tongue.

Someone called for an ambulance. While we waited, we tried to talk to him and keep him from hurting himself, but he continued to thrash and foam at the mouth. When the ambulance arrived, he was put on a stretcher, strapped down, and given a sedative. I got in the back with him, together with a hospital attendant. On the way to the hospital he continued to thrash and foam at the mouth, but not severely. At the hospital I was told that Jones had combat fatigue and would not be returned to combat.

The Oxford American Dictionary defines combat fatigue as a "mental disorder due to stress in wartime combat." The only other cases of possible combat fatigue that I saw occurred in the Hürtgen Forest. The first case involved a man who, during a long and heavy German artillery barrage, cried uncontrollably in his log-covered foxhole. I don't think that his crying was the sign of any mental disorder but was a sane response to a terrifying situation. I, and the other men around him, probably felt like crying, but we didn't

The second concerned a man who lay on the open ground screaming, crying, and pounding the earth while the Germans were plastering the area with mortar fire. The rest of us had found the relative safety of foxholes. This man was not acting rationally because he jeopardized his life by his behavior. I don't know if he suffered from a mental disorder, but I don't believe he had any comparable experience later. Both of these men had been under fire daily for more than a week. What caused them to break down was surely the cumulative effect of the constant pounding of the artillery over a period of days as well as the immediate shelling they were experiencing.

The sights and sounds of combat got to everyone sooner or later. I think I tolerated the experiences of combat as well as most, but I remember, months after I had returned home from the war, on a number of occasions crouching low and preparing to hit the ground upon hearing the whistling of a low-flying airplane, which sounded like an incoming artillery shell. For months, and possibly years, after returning home, I would catch myself subconsciously, and consciously, trying to determine how best to attack a building or hill I happened to encounter. I don't know if that's combat fatigue, but I suppose that all combat infantrymen suffer "mental disorder due to stress." The difference between Jones and the rest of us was a matter of how and when the symptoms of mental disorder were manifested.

As to Jones, I never saw him again. And the Third Army's huge attack mentioned earlier didn't take place.

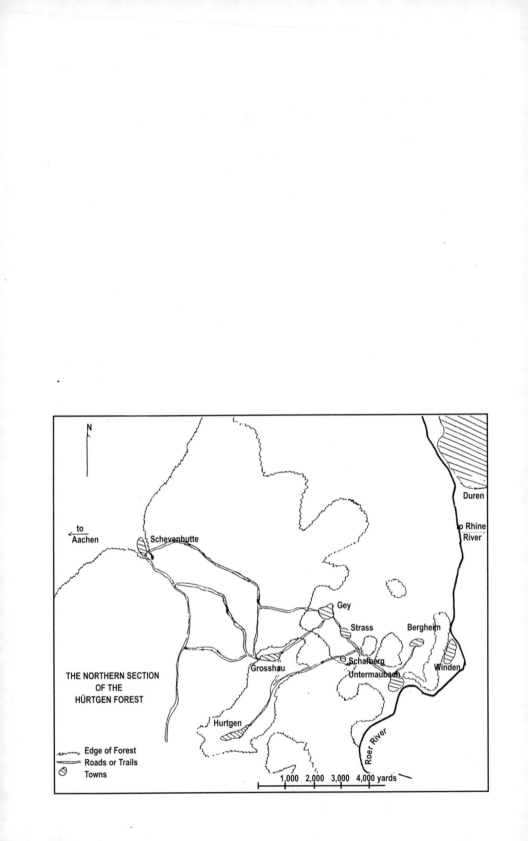

N

to
Aachen

Schevenhutte

Duren

to Rhine
River

Gey

Strass

Bergheim

Schafberg

THE NORTHERN SECTION
OF THE
HÜRTGEN FOREST

Grosshau

Untermaubach

Winden

Hurtgen

Roer River

Edge of Forest
Roads or Trails
Towns

1,000 2,000 3,000 4,000 yards

Chapter Five

Hürtgen Forest - Part One
December 1944

*"East of Aachen troops of the First Army fought splen-
didly through bloody Hürtgen Forest, taking casualties
and inflicting heavy losses on the stubborn enemy."*[5]

I N LATE NOVEMBER, WE RECEIVED orders to move to the Hürtgen Forest. Until that time, the war hadn't seemed very
real or very deadly to me, but I was anxious to learn what
combat was like. I wanted to be in enough combat to have the
experience, probably to be able to talk about it after I got home.
I wondered how I would behave and react, and I'm sure I had
an underlying fear that I might turn out to be a coward. After
a very few days in the Hürtgen, I had acquired enough combat
experience to last me several lifetimes.

The Hürtgen Forest lies east of Aachen, a city just east
of the Dutch border. It was the first German city taken by the
Allied forces in the war. The American First Division fought
through and captured Aachen in September and October of
1944. At about the same time, American troops entered the
Hürtgen Forest. The battle that followed was one of the bloodiest of the war.[6]

---

[5]General Marshall's Report, *The Winning of the War in Europe and the Pacific*,
p. 42.

[6]The U.S. Army suffered 25,000 to 30,000 killed or wounded in action, plus
several thousand hospitalized with trench foot, combat fatigue, or other ill-
nesses.

In the fall of 1944, the British, American, Canadian, French, and other Allied forces were attempting to drive into Germany from the west and thus end the war. The Russians on the east were still many miles from the German border. The Americans, in one sector, were attacking toward the Roer River, which lay about twenty miles east of Aachen. Across the Roer lay the Cologne Plain, which is relatively flat land where we thought we could take advantage of our superiority in numbers of tanks. But the land west of the Roer had to be captured first. It was hillier, rougher countryside, not well suited to the massive use of tanks. The Hürtgen Forest (Hürtgenwald in German) was part of the area between Aachen and the Roer.

The Hürtgen was heavily wooded with tall pine trees. They were so dense that even when the sun shone, the day seemed gray. On cloudy days, everything was still more gray. The forest measures about ten by twenty miles. Some historians have said that the Americans should have bypassed the Hürtgen, because the terrain did not allow us to use our tanks and air force to best advantage, leaving the infantry to suffer unnecessarily heavy casualties. The Germans were surprised that we attacked through it. They thought that we could have made better use of our resources elsewhere, for the same reasons mentioned above. In the Hürtgen, they were able to tie up a large number of our forces without the use of their best troops, while they concentrated their panzer and other elite units to the south for action in the Battle of the Bulge. Of course, hindsight is always twenty-twenty, but if the Germans thought it was a mistake for us to conduct such a large campaign there, we probably should not have.

Possibly an even more convincing argument as to why the Americans should not have attacked through the Hürtgen is the failure of the American leaders to consider the Roer River dams located a short distance upriver (south) from the Hürtgen.

The U.S. Army entered the Hürtgen in order to break through to the Roer River. The plan was to cross the Roer to the Cologne Plain and then to proceed on to the Rhine. At the beginning of the Hürtgen campaign, the American leaders either did not know of the existence of the dams or, if they knew of them, did not understand their importance. If the Americans got to the Roer, the Germans could release the water in the dams and flood the river valley. It was, therefore, vital that the Americans should seize control of the dams. But the American high command decided to push through the Hürtgen and at least temporarily to ignore the dams, resulting in the appalling American casualties. The wise strategy would have been to stay out of the Hürtgen and attack to the south of it and get to the Roer and the dams in the same operation.

Stephen E. Ambrose, in his book, *Citizen Soldiers*, clearly points out the mistake the American high command made by attacking through the Hürtgen: "The forest could have been bypassed to the south, with the dams the objective. The forest without the dams was worthless; the dams without the forest was priceless. But the generals got it backwards, and went for the forest. Thus did the Battle of Hürtgen get started on the basis of a plan that was grossly, even criminally stupid."

Self-criticism is an undertaking most of us do not practice. I think this is especially true of the American Army's top brass concerning the Hürtgen Forest battle. In the head note at the beginning of this chapter, the report of General Marshall states, ". . . the First Army *fought splendidly* through bloody Hürtgen Forest, *taking casualties* . . ." (emphasis added) Whoever wrote that should have been there. My recollection—of one of my men who died from an artillery shell that tore off the top of his head or of another man who died when a large chunk of red-hot shrapnel created a hole the size of my fist when it slammed into his chest—does not fit the characterization of "fought splendidly" or "taking casualties."

Such military jargon by the U.S. Army's top brass serves to defuse and cover up the suffering and deaths of thousands of young American men who were maimed or killed in the full flower of their lives. Pretty language does not truly honor the sacrifices made by the men in that seldom heard of, death-filled forest. I have read the books written by Generals Dwight

D. Eisenhower and Omar Bradley[7] in which they wrote of their wartime experiences. I recall no hint from them that the Hürtgen campaign was a mistake from the beginning. I saw nothing to indicate, after the first few weeks in the Hürtgen, where we had suffered thousands of casualties, that the brass considered halting the attack and directing our efforts elsewhere. Instead they compounded their mistake by throwing more men into the forest, with the result of thousands more casualties.

Our actions in the Hürtgen remind me of the losses incurred in the British army in World War I in the First Battle of the Somme. The British top brass brought on the deaths of thousands of Britain's finest young men in a fruitless effort to end the war. They kept sending in more and more men to replace the heavy losses incurred in the fighting, resulting in horrible casualties numbering in the tens of thousands.

Back to the Hürtgen. The Germans were dug into defensive positions with logs covering their foxholes. When the German artillery and mortar shells would hit the tops of the trees, the "tree bursts," as they were called, caused unusually heavy casualties to the soldiers below. Of course American artillery caused tree bursts over the Germans as well, but the Germans were usually defending, not attacking. They were able to protect themselves by crawling into their log-covered foxholes. When you are attacking, you can't bring a foxhole with you.

An artillery or mortar shell which lands on the ground (a ground burst) explodes on contact, causing the shrapnel to go in all directions, including into the ground. Thus, some of the shrapnel in a ground burst goes into the ground, and does

---

[7]Omar N. Bradley (1893 to 1981) was commander of the U.S. 12th Army Group in Europe when World War II ended. He was a full general at the time. In 1951, his book, *A Soldier's Story*, was published, covering his experiences in the war. Dwight D. Eisenhower (1890 to 1969) was Supreme Commander, Allied Expeditionary Forces in Europe when the war ended. He was a "General of the Army" at the time. In 1948, his book, *Crusade in Europe*, was published, covering his experiences in the war. From 1953 to 1961, he served as thirty-fourth president of the United States.

not hit anybody. But all of the shrapnel in a tree burst cuts through the air, increasing the chance of hitting someone. When an artillery shell is fired in your direction, it makes a whistling noise. Upon hearing it, we would hit the ground. If the shell landed on the ground, it would explode and the shrapnel would fly in an arc from impact over the prostrate bodies of the intended victims. Of course, if you were unlucky enough to be lying either at the point of impact or at one of the places where the shrapnel landed, you could be hurt or killed. On the other hand, if the shell hit a tree, the tree burst would send hot shrapnel downward and outward, dispersing it over the entire area beneath the point of impact—over an area of perhaps fifty to 250 feet in diameter, depending on the size of the shell. Therefore, the poor fellow who hit the ground before the explosion—and exposed his whole body flat on the ground—was much more likely to be hit if there were a tree burst rather than a ground burst.

I have heard that some men, in order to avoid being hit by a tree burst, would stand up next to a tree rather than fall to the ground, to avoid the shrapnel from above. I don't know if that procedure was ever tried, and, if so, whether it worked. I suppose that a man would have to decide, even before he heard a shell coming in, whether to stand against a tree or to hit the ground. That meant predicting that there would or would not be a tree burst and then having the courage to stand up while a shell exploded nearby. As for me, I had neither the skills nor the inclination to do this, although it never occurred to me to try. My personal technique was to hit the ground fast and hard, praying all the while.

Besides the trees, my first impression of the Hürtgen was the unremitting noise of the artillery. It sounded like a thunderstorm that went on and on without stopping. I had heard enemy artillery before, in Luxembourg, but that was a mere spring shower compared to the deluge of the Hürtgen. I felt that I was getting into the real thing.

Eight or nine American divisions had been fighting there off and on for two months, and they had suffered terrible casualties. E Company replaced a company from the Fourth Division. My most vivid memory of the men from the Fourth is the light-colored mud caked on their uniforms and faces. They looked like a collection of ghosts. The weather was between thirty and forty degrees Fahrenheit, and there was frequent cold rain or light snow, so the ground was often damp or muddy. When you sleep in a muddy foxhole with no facilities to wash or bathe and have no fresh clothes, you soon look dirty and ghostlike. The men of the Fourth had been in the forest several weeks and well over half of those who entered had been killed or wounded. They were a grim lot, hollow-eyed from the constant pounding of shellfire and the fear of impending death. They reminded me of zombies—the risen dead.

Most of the trees had their tops knocked off from the tree bursts. Others had been hit close to the base of the trunk with the result that the greatest part of the tree lay on the ground attached to the trunk. The remaining trees were disfigured by the scars of shrapnel, and craters dotted the terrain where shells had gotten through and burst on the ground.

My platoon moved into the positions held by a Fourth Division platoon. The area was heavily wooded with pine and had thick underbrush in some places. Adding to the difficulty in walking were the fallen tree tops, which we had to walk around or climb over.

The Fourth Division men showed us their positions, where their automatic weapons were located, and the fields of fire for all the weapons, as well as the Germans' general location. They also told us whatever else they knew, such as what kind of activity both they and the Germans had recently undertaken. There hadn't been much.

Rather than stay in these original positions where we were subjected continuously to the German artillery fire, why didn't we attack immediately or at least pull back out of range or sight of the German artillery? Since I was about a dozen notches below those who made the decisions, I can only speculate. The 83rd was replacing the Fourth, and it must have taken some time to plan and coordinate an attack, so a delay would seem to be quite natural. Pulling back might seem to have been a logical move, but what if the Germans then advanced into the area we just vacated? The Hürtgen property was too dearly purchased wih American lives. To risk having to take it a second time was unthinkable.

A "field of fire" is the area in front of one's position where fire is directed toward an advancing enemy. Ideally, a field of fire will be a large flat open area, free of hills and depressions, free of cover (trees and other solid objects that could stop small arms fire) and free of concealment (shrubbery and other things that would not stop a bullet but would conceal the enemy's approach). Since the area in front of our positions was filled with trees, underbrush, and irregular ground, it is hard to imagine a poorer field of fire.

We used the foxholes which the Fourth Division men had dug, and added some of our own. They were two to four feet deep with logs on top and large enough to accommodate two or three men. The foxholes were arranged roughly in a half circle facing the Germans. The forest was so thick that I never did see exactly where the Germans were, but they were somewhere ahead of us. The Fourth Division had taken the ground and then dug into the area they held, awaiting further orders.

When we arrived, there were several dead German soldiers lying on the ground. They had the ashen complexion of the dead, but they were not swollen nor decomposed nor bad-smelling, as they would have been had the weather been warm. They lay where they had fallen, some face down and others face up, staring skyward. The presence of the dead bodies didn't bother me much, probably because of more pressing worries, such as the constant shelling. After a few days, they just became part of the landscape. They were heavily dressed in the gray-blue winter uniform of the German army, so I don't remember seeing any marks on their bodies which would indicate where they had been hit or by what kind of projectile.

We didn't touch the bodies because we had heard that the Germans booby-trapped everything, so we were afraid of moving the dead and having them blow up in our faces. From the time I joined E Company, everyone was repeatedly warned to beware of booby traps. The men who had fought in Normandy were very cautious about them, and my impression was that some of those men had seen the fatal effects of German booby traps. I didn't have any personal experience with them, and, if I had, I probably wouldn't be here today.

We stayed in our positions for about a week, and we spent our time trying to stay alive. The men kept close to their foxholes because the German artillery fire was so frequent that they were afraid of being far from protection when it started.

We didn't ever have hot food while in those positions. There was no road to us, so the mess sergeant and his men, or a carrying party from the platoon, would have had to carry the heavy, hot food containers several hundred yards to reach us. The bad part was not carrying the food but the risk of being caught in the open if the German big guns opened up.

We ate K rations, which came in boxes about the size of a large Cracker Jack box. (Incidentally, the K ration was the brain child of a fellow Minnesotan, Dr. Ancel Keys, of the University of Minnesota Medical School.) Each man received three boxes of K rations each day, labeled Breakfast, Lunch, and Dinner. Each box contained a small can of processed meat, cheese, or cooked eggs, crackers, dried fruit, a beverage in the form of powdered soup, coffee, or lemonade, as well as chewing gum, candy, and cigarettes, and, finally, toilet paper—a most vital item of equipment. After a week or two of K rations, a hot meal became a real treat.

If I were asked what was the most important piece of equipment that a soldier could carry, I think my answer would be toilet paper. To assure a ready supply at all times, I always carried caches of it in two places—one in the inside of the top of my helmet liner, and the second in my upper left shirt pocket. Perhaps my greatest, and possibly only, accomplishment during the war was that my toilet paper system worked perfectly, and I never failed to have the important stuff when it was needed.

As soon as we arrived at our original positions, I set out trip flares in a little unoccupied valley which lay to the left of our position. One or two of my men and I strung wire along the ground with flares attached. If the Germans tried to attack through the valley in the dark, they would, we hoped, trip on the wire and light up the flares so we would be alerted to their movement. I had never worked with flares before this, so I still don't know if I set them up properly. Fortunately, the Germans didn't test my flare-setting skills.

Our chief fear was the German artillery. As soon as we heard the whistle of artillery coming in, we would jump into a log covered foxhole. The artillery would last for several minutes while we lay flat in the foxhole, hoping that we would not receive a direct hit. If you thought too much about this, you could fall apart emotionally from the strain. As you lay there, the shells would shake your body when they hit close by. The noise from the exploding shells is probably the most frightening thing on the receiving end of artillery fire. While the shells were coming in, I'm sure that I promised God frequently that I would be a better person in the future, if only He would let me live.

I have a theory that the infantry leaders (corporals, sergeants, lieutenants, and captains) might not have been as frightened by the sounds and stress of battle as the other men because the leaders had duties to perform so they could not spend all their time worrying about their own safety. During a firefight, and to a lesser degree when being bombarded by enemy artillery, the leader would often be distracted from concern about himself by the necessity of planning what to do next.

Ma Bell - Army Style

One of the most dangerous jobs while we were in the original positions was walking the telephone lines to find the break in the wire caused by German shellfire. In order to communicate with company headquarters, a telephone line was laid on the ground from the company C.P. (command post) to the platoon C.P. We also had a small SCR536 radio (a walkie-talkie) to talk to the company C.P. The telephone was clearer and more reliable than the radio, so we used the telephone when we were not on the move. The main drawback of the telephone was that the line would go dead when a German shell severed the wire. When this happened, Bonnet or I would send someone out to find the break in the wire and repair it. This was a rotten assignment, for no one knew when the German fire would start again and catch the wire man in the open with the tree bursts and no protection against the flying shrapnel. The telephone lines had to be walked several times each day, and I would guess that a fourth of the casualties incurred by the company while in the original positions were suffered by the wire men. I'm sure that all the men dreaded the telephone line repair assignment, but I don't recall anyone complaining or hesitating to do the job. There probably was plenty of complaining, but not within earshot of me. The old army way was to complain about everything. If it was worth doing, it was worth complaining about.

Direct or Indirect Fire

Which type of fire would I have preferred to have directed at me, machine gun or artillery? That's like asking a man if he would prefer falling off a high bridge or a tall building.

I prefer "none of the above," but since I'm asking the question and demanding an answer of myself, I'm inclined to say that direct fire (machine gun, rifle, and burp gun) frightened me less than indirect fire (artillery and mortar). You could usually see where the direct fire was coming from and could, therefore, try to do something about it, such as firing toward it or attacking the enemy position. You could stay busy trying to eliminate the enemy's direct fire and, thereby, be distracted from the fear of it. Or you could get behind something that would afford protection. In contrast, when on the receiving end of artillery and mortar fire, all one could do was hug the ground and hope and pray that it would stop soon and you would not be killed. The feeling while suffering through the crashing of artillery and mortar shells was complete helplessness. It was like being in an airplane during turbulent weather when the plane is bouncing up and down and then hits an air pocket and drops suddenly and seems to be out of control of the pilot and, of course, yourself.

Ernest Elliott was my radio man and runner. He had been wounded in Normandy and rejoined us in the Hürtgen, so I had only known him for a few days. He was from Indiana and was probably twenty years old, but appeared younger to me. His average height and somewhat slight build helped him in one of the qualifications for runner, which was to run. And he could run. But more important, he was a bright fellow who was not afraid to enlighten me with his opinion on anything that came up. Although he was a PFC and I a lieutenant, he was never hesitant to let me know what he thought or what he would do. For example, he might say to me, even if I had not asked for his opinion, "Lieutenant, I wouldn't be too soft on _____, he's always been a gold bricker and will do whatever it takes to duck real work." I was not accustomed to such forthright talk, but I enjoyed it as a contrast to the fairly formal relationship I had with the other men in the platoon.

The German artillery came in many times each day, but more frightening was shelling at night. Lying in a hole in the pitch black of night with shells bursting all around was terrifying.

One night, during a blistering barrage of several minutes, one of my men in an adjoining foxhole called to me to come to his hole. "Lieutenant," he called, "will you come over here?"

"Yeah, what d'ya want?" I said.

"It's Smith. Can you talk to him?"

"Okay. Just a second," I said as I put on my helmet.

I waited until the shelling let up a little and then got out of my hole and ran the thirty or so feet over to Smith (not his real name) who was crying uncontrollably. I crawled into his hole and tried to comfort him. There was no need for me to ask what was wrong. I was going through the same terrible shell fire as he. But neither I nor anyone else could do anything about it. Smith was sobbing like a toddler who had just lost his mother in a crowded shopping mall.

He wanted to get out of there. We *all* wanted to get out of there, but some people can take the strain of shelling better than others. Obviously, most of us were able to withstand it better than he. I sat next to him in the foxhole and held him in my arms as if he were my child. I tried to give some comfort by talking and just holding him. There were no courses at St. Thomas or Fort Benning that covered this situation. I had no special words with which to comfort him. But I don't think the words I said were important. The important thing for that man was to know that he was with friends who cared for him and were in the same boat as he.

I said, "Smith, just take it easy. You'll be all right."

"Lieutenant, I can't take it anymore. I've got to get out of here."

"Well, Smith, we all want to get out of here, but we can't. It'll let up soon."

"Lieutenant, I just can't take it any more. Get me out of here."

"Smith, if we tried to go now, we couldn't get fifty feet. Just hang on, and we'll make it. It can't keep up like this much longer."

"Lieutenant, get me out of here!"

After about a half hour, he quieted down, and I returned to my hole. As far as I know, he never again had a similar episode.

Breakfast (Not) in Bed

Early one morning, I received a telephone call from Chambers, the company commander.

"Devitt, this is Chambers. How'd it go last night?"

"Okay, sir. We had a lot of incoming, but no casualties."

"That's good. Say, I want ya'll to report back here at the C.P. right away."

"What's up?" I said. "I'd rather not go back right now. The Krauts haven't come through with their early morning barrage yet, and I don't want to get caught out in the open between foxholes."

"Oh, ya'll make it all right. Come right now."

I realized that arguing further would be fruitless, so I said, "Willco. Roger. Out," in army communication's jargon.

Company headquarters was only about two hundred yards behind my position, but because of the fallen trees and the underbrush, the walk back would take about fifteen minutes, rather than five over better terrain. Being fifteen minutes away from a foxhole was a very frightening prospect.

But my worry was unnecessary. I got back to company headquarters safely and was greeted cheerily by Chambers. The other platoon leaders were also there. Chambers said with a broad smile, "Hi, Devitt. Glad ya'll made it. You're just in time for breakfast. Have some coffee. Oh, yeah, ya'll don't drink coffee. Well there's water in that Jerri-can."

"Thanks a lot, sir," I said. "It was a nice walk."

For the first time in several days, the mess sergeant was able to get hot food to company headquarters, so Chambers thought it would be a treat for us to share it. I could have strangled him for inviting me. Although I enjoyed the hot food, it was not worth the risk. That could have been the most expensive meal of my life—or the last one.

I don't recall what we had to eat, but a typical breakfast would have been pancakes and bacon with lots of hot coffee (except for me) and perhaps some canned grapefruit to let the menu makers give tribute to a balanced diet.

Several times daily I went to each foxhole in the platoon to check on the men. There was little to do but try to stay as safe and comfortable as possible. The men spent their days eating K rations, cleaning their weapons, changing their socks, keeping a lookout for the Germans, washing, rubbing their feet to prevent trench foot, getting water, improving their holes, and lying face down in their foxholes, hugging the ground during the frequent death-laden German artillery fire. In making the rounds, I would usually go with Bonnet and Elliott. The men would be in or close to their holes because of the constant threat of the German big guns.

One day while I was making my rounds with Bonnet and Elliott, the German artillery started firing. Everybody quickly got into foxholes. When the shelling stopped I looked out and saw two wounded American soldiers on the ground not far away. They were from an adjoining company and had come to our position to make contact with us. When the artillery fire started, they apparently could not find a foxhole, or else they were hit before they could get into one.

I immediately went over to one of the men who was lying on his back. As I knelt over him, I saw that he had a large hole the size of my fist in his chest just below his right shoulder. A big chunk of red hot shrapnel had caught him there. The stench of burning flesh almost made me retch. His eyes were closed, and he was unconscious. His skin was turning a yellowish color, his breathing was heavy, and he was gasping for air.

The other man was about ten feet away with his back against a tree. He had been hit in both legs but was able to see what was going on.

"Bonnet," I shouted, "Call company and tell 'em to send two litters with carrying crews. Tell 'em we've got two men who are hit bad. Get a medic down here right away."

"Okay, Lieutenant," Bonnet said. He immediately ran to the platoon C.P. and called the company C.P.

I started to put a bandage on the first man's chest. This was especially difficult to do. First, the sight of the large hole in his chest and the smell of the burning flesh were formidable. Smoke or steam arose from the wound, and its location on his body made it difficult to find a way to tie a bandage.

I was alone with the two wounded men, since my men had stayed in their foxholes, fearful that the German artillery might begin again.

About the time I got the bandage on, four men appeared with a litter and asked which wounded man should go first. I thought to myself why didn't they send two litters, but I didn't say anything. While I was putting the bandage on the first man, the second kept saying "Lieutenant, he won't make it. Come and help me." So when the litter arrived I had to decide which to take first. I felt that the only chance the first man had of surviving was to get immediate help. So we put him on the litter. The second repeated, "Lieutenant, take me. He can't make it."

Nevertheless, we took the first man. He was now breathing faintly, and the going was very slow. Although there were five of us carrying the litter, it was very hard work because we had to lift the litter over and under the fallen trees. All this time we knew that the German artillery might open up at any moment. After we had gone about fifty yards, the injured man suddenly shuddered, and I saw that he was dead. We rolled him onto the ground and went back for the second man, whom we were able to evacuate without incident.

I recently retold this story to my oldest son, Christopher. When I had finished, he said, "You were a hero!" I told him, with perhaps excess modesty, "No," for that was the job of an infantry leader. Things that others got medals for, the front-line infantryman did every day. I told Chris the story of a major I knew who was in the quartermaster corps, who received a Silver Star medal for bravery in leading a convoy of trucks under artillery fire. I told Chris that, although I didn't doubt that the major was brave and deserved the Silver Star, the action for which he received it was the sort of thing infantrymen experienced with regularity, usually without getting medals. There simply was no comparison between the risks and privations suffered by the front-line infantryman and the non-combat soldiers.

The definition of a front-line infantryman depended on who was doing the defining. To most of us in the rifle platoons, anyone not in a unit like ours was rear echelon. That was not a chauvinistic position to take. If, for example, someone from company headquarters had a small hill or building between himself and our platoon, which was under fired by the enemy, he was immeasurably safer than we were. On the other hand,

I suspect that the lead scouts in the rifle platoons often thought that they were fighting the war all by themselves, and that all others, including the rest of the rifle platoons, were rear echelon.

There were probably four supporting troops for every front-line infantryman. In talking to a veteran of World War II, one will sometimes hear him say with pride in his voice, "I was in Patton's Third Army." The question that should be asked of that veteran is, "What was your job?" The chances are that he was never or seldom near any enemy fire.

Goofy

Another incident showed me that a person won't always behave the way one would think he will. The man involved was called Goofy by the men. He earned the nickname by his eccentric behavior, the most extreme example of which occurred during a training exercise in which he fired a round of live ammunition past the battalion commander, who was inspecting at the time. He was not even supposed to have had live ammunition, let alone fire it. In retrospect, this seems like a cruel name to call somebody, but I don't think that anybody called him that to his face. I thought that, after we got into combat, Goofy would be the first to crack under the pressure.

One day in the Hürtgen, while I was visiting the men in the foxholes, the German artillery opened up. I jumped into the nearest hole and found that it was occupied by Goofy and another man. The other man and I lay in the hole and tried to stay calm. Shells were exploding near our hole, throwing dirt and shrapnel into the air, and shaking us from the force of the concussion. I was very frightened, and was trying to stop thinking of what would happen if a shell landed too close. Goofy's reaction was not what I expected. Instead of crying or becoming hysterical, Goofy talked calmly to us, and seemed oblivious to the shelling.

"Look, Lieutenant," he said, "it ain't as bad as it was this morning. We've got a good hole here, and we added more logs on top yesterday. It'll take a direct hit to get us, and we ain't had one in the whole platoon yet. There ain't much to be afraid of."

"I hope you're right," I said.

I realize now that I had badly misjudged him.

Chief

One of the men in the third platoon was an American Indian, who was called Chief by the other men. He was a very quiet fellow who did his job well without indulging in loud talk or any talk at all. When we arrived in the Hürtgen, I thought that Chief would be in his element in the outdoors living on the cold ground. One day we saw that Chief was shivering from the cold and that he had a high fever. We sent him back to the battalion aid station where he was diagnosed with pneumonia and then hospitalized. At the time this surprised me, for I assumed that an Indian must have been accustomed to living outdoors and, therefore, would be immune from an illness such as pneumonia. The truth probably was that Chief had not spent any more time outdoors during his life, nor had any more immunity from disease, than I had. It would have been just as logical to assume that I should have carried a shillelagh since I'm Irish. Before writing this (and using the dictionary) I couldn't even spell shillelagh, let alone own or carry one.

E Company suffered thirty-six casualties during the week or so it occupied the original positions in the Hürtgen, all caused by German artillery and mortar fire before we had any contact with the Germans on the ground.[8] One casualty was Vitulo, the second platoon leader.

Haney and Vitulo

F.M. Haney was a technical sergeant and platoon sergeant of E Company's second platoon. He later was promoted to first sergeant of the company. Vitulo was a second

[8] These figures were given to me by Troy Wooldridge, who was first sergeant of E Company during that period.

lieutenant, who took command of the second platoon at the same time I was appointed leader of the third. Haney was the leader of the second platoon when Vitulo arrived, having taken over in Normandy after the departure of the lieutenant who had been its leader previously. He probably was killed or wounded. Haney's situation was similar to Bonnet's, a veteran combat sergeant being replaced by a lieutenant with no battle experience. Haney, from Alabama, a seasoned combat veteran, exuded the confidence that he had earned from his battle experiences, attested to by his Silver Star medal and four Purple Hearts, one of which he received for a wound suffered in the Hürtgen.

Bonnet and I got along with each other and liked each other quite well, but the same was not true of Haney and Vitulo. (Perhaps Vitulo should have given Haney his liquor ration.) When we were in training, Vitulo would sometimes complain to me privately about Haney, but I never understood his complaints. I think there was simply a clash of personalities. Vitulo, being the new leader of the platoon, wanted to assert himself and let the men know that he was in charge, whereas Haney, the former leader, wanted to be able to use his know-how and experience to the fullest. He probably felt that he had done a good job and should not have been replaced.

One day, after being in the Hürtgen only a day or two, Haney walked by Vitulo's foxhole and noted that Vitulo did not have many logs covering it. Haney said, "Lieutenant, you'd better get some more logs over that hole. You don't have much protection now. One of those tree bursts could cause you a lot of trouble. I'll get an axe."

"Thanks, Haney, but don't bother. I'll take care of it," Vitulo replied.

Haney went to his hole, and soon after a German artillery barrage started. After it ended, Haney went back to Vitulo and found that he had been hit. He was wounded slightly in one hand by shrapnel, but he might not have been hit if he had had more cover over him. Upon realizing that he was not hurt badly, Vitulo knew that he would be taken out of that deadly forest and away from the constant threat of instant death. He jumped out of his hole and waved his injured hand, happily announcing with a big smile, "Look Haney, here's my ticket home. Talk about a million-dollar wound, this is it. Call the medic to put on a bandage. Then it's to the rear for me. I've had enough of this place."

Haney, and Bonnet, too, who had never seen anyone react to a wound in such a light-hearted way, thought that Vitulo's behavior was inappropriate, even peculiar. I think that Vitulo's actions were very understandable considering the circumstances. It might be suggested that he did not act the way a good leader should. I disagree. Vitulo was wounded and was no longer a leader. He was out of it. He was merely expressing in his own way his joy in leaving, something that anyone with an ounce of brains would see as a good thing.

Wooldridge

Troy Wooldridge was first sergeant of E Company when I joined it in Dinard. He was in his late twenties, but he seemed older to me. Being a career soldier, he believed in obedience and discipline, and as first sergeant he was the highest ranking enlisted man in the company. He had power and authority, and everyone in the company knew it. When he gave an order, there was no question that he expected immediate compliance. He was a pretty big man, at least he seemed so to me, so his orders were not treated lightly. Although I outranked him, technically that is, and was not subject to his orders, I nevertheless felt a certain amount of fear in his presence. I suppose that I felt that he could see through my façade of being an experienced soldier, especially since he had ten years of army experience compared to my two.

To me the peak of his power was reached after we had been in the Hürtgen a few days and could not shave. Wooldridge grew a thick, black beard, which made him appear like the captain of a pirate ship. All he needed was a red bandanna around his head to complete the picture. I think his appear-

F. M. Haney (left) and Walter Bonnet, platoon sergeants of the second and third platoons of E Company near a German dugout in Dinard. Haney, with a Thompson sub-machine gun, appears ready to fight. I'm glad that he and Bonnet were on our side. Fall 1944. (Photo by author)

ance alone frightened many a rookie soldier, including one rookie second lieutenant.

Chewing Gum

While in the Hürtgen, we ate K rations three times a day. In each ration were two or three cigarettes and a stick or two of gum. Powdered coffee was in only one of the rations, and this was usually the only coffee available. Since I didn't smoke or drink coffee, I always gave those items to the men in my platoon. However, I did chew gum, as much as I could find. After about a week of K rations, Marty Martinson, the Minnesota boy, presented me with a package of about thirty sticks of gum which he had saved from his K rations, using a cellophane package that had contained crackers. I'm sure that I had given Marty cigarettes and powdered coffee, but no more than I had given to others. In the midst of the daily risks of combat and the almost constant fear of death, he had taken the trouble to save a stick or two of gum for me each time he ate. I was touched by his thoughtfulness, and even now, I am near tears writing about it.

Trenchfoot

I first heard of trenchfoot from reports of the Italian campaign in the winter of 1943-1944. This is a condition that affects the feet when they are subjected to cold and dampness over an extended period of time. It ranged in seriousness from minor discomfort in the feet to amputation of toes or feet. My two big toes have been numb since 1945, the result of being cold and wet constantly in the Hürtgen Forest. The more serious manifestations of this condition were swelling and pain in the feet together with lack of circulation. Walking became painful, and men were often hospitalized, and sometimes a foot was amputated because of infection.

Sometime after I joined E Company, everyone in the company received instructions from on high as to how to protect against trenchfoot. We were all issued an extra pair of socks and were told to change them every day. The old wet and dirty socks were to be dried by putting them around our waists, where the heat from our bodies would dry them. In addition, we were each to have a buddy who would help us take care of our feet. Each buddy would rub the feet of his counterpart every day, to maintain the circulation in the feet.

I don't know who thought of this procedure, but I think that he had in mind a girls' finishing school rather than the Hürtgen Forest. I never had a buddy for the trenchfoot exercise, and if I had, I don't believe that I would have rubbed the dirty, smelly feet of a fellow soldier no matter how concerned I might have been for his podiatric well-being.

Whoever devised this foot-rubbing procedure probably had never been in combat. In my combat experiences, men were wounded and hospitalized almost every day. Imagine someone whose buddy had been evacuated spending time inquiring who else had lost a buddy so that the two could join up to form a new foot-rubbing team. Maybe the American soldiers in the Italian campaign had the time and inclination to do this, but my men and I did not, so we took care of our own feet the best we could. I changed my socks and rubbed my feet frequently and that was the way all of our men took care of theirs.

Equipment

For a fellow who sometimes can't remember his telephone number, it would be unrealistic of me to expect to list accurately the equipment I carried in combat, but I'll try. I kept on my back a musette bag, which was a canvas back pack which contained a toothbrush and toothpaste, shaving equipment, soap, a towel, socks, underwear, extra ammunition, and K rations. We had all been issued gas masks, but because the Germans had not used gas, we left the masks in storage when we went up on the line. Attached to the cartridge belt, which was held up with suspenders, were a canteen with water, a compass, an entrenching shovel, a small first-aid kit including a bandage, a knife, and extra clips of ammunition. Hand grenades were usually attached to rings on the suspenders. Although as an officer I had been issued a carbine, when I got into combat I carried the M-1 rifle, which all other men (except the automatic riflemen) in the platoon carried. I made this switch in weapons probably because some experienced combat veteran told me that I would be less likely to be recognized as an officer by the enemy if I carried the same weapon as the rest.

Chapter Six

Hürtgen Forest - Part Two
December 1944

Attack in the Woods

A FTER ABOUT A WEEK in the original positions, we were ordered to move. The morning we moved, we went through a gully called Bloody Gulch, through which other Americans had attacked a few days earlier. The early morning sun was just appearing when we walked into the ravine. As I first entered it, I stumbled over something in the dim light. I looked down and saw it was the body of an American soldier. As I walked on, the increasing light showed an American body every few yards. When the Americans had attacked through the gully, the Germans were able to fire into it and kill them. Because of the danger and difficulty in moving in the Hürtgen, the American Graves Registration people were unable to get the bodies out until after we had been there.

The light was so dim that I couldn't see the faces of the dead American soldiers over whom I was stepping. If I had seen their faces, I'm sure that the unblinking stare emerging from the death pallor would have moved me greatly. I was not particularly affected by their presence, probably because I did not see the faces and particularly because, within the last week, I had seen a large number of dead soldiers, both American and German. I was getting hardened to the sight of death.

After passing through Bloody Gulch, we proceeded through the woods toward the German lines. The company was walking through the woods in an approach march formation, with the first and second platoons in front and mine, the third, in reserve in the rear. Although this was my first close contact with the German infantry, I was not unduly worried or frightened, probably because, as is really true, ignorance is bliss.

Suddenly German small arms fire was directed against the first platoon. The men immediately hit the ground and returned the fire. My platoon was closely behind the first.

The Germans were only twenty-five yards away from the first platoon. After it had been pinned down by the Germans for about ten minutes, Sandler, the platoon leader, called to his men, "Come on, let's get 'em." He jumped up, and after he took only a step or two, a German rifleman shot him through the head. Sandler's men, who were still on the ground, arose together, as if by a signal, and rushed the Germans. It was over in a minute. The first platoon overwhelmed the German position, just like in the movies. Sandler, the Lithuanian Jew, had died heroically but probably without any formal recognition such as a Silver Star for bravery. But he had earned, and received, something even more valuable to an infantry leader— the love and admiration of his men.

A few minutes after Sandler's death, the Germans began a heavy mortar barrage on the company. Everyone immediately sought some sort of hole or ditch for protection. I jumped into a good sized foxhole, which had been dug by some earlier German or American excavator, but three of my men were quicker than I, so I jumped in on top of them. After getting untangled from the others, I heard someone screaming hysterically. I looked out and saw one of my men lying on the ground, face down, crying and yelling and pounding the earth. The mortar shells continued to land. He obviously couldn't last long where he was, so I got out of the hole and ran over to him, a distance of ten or fifteen feet. I reached down and grabbed one of his arms and said, "Come on. Let's go."

He couldn't, or wouldn't, get up by himself, so I dragged him like a big sack of potatoes over to the hole and threw him in and jumped on top of him. The hole was so packed that my man might have preferred that I'd left him out in the open to take his chances.

As soon as the mortar fire let up, Chambers, seeing that the Germans knew our exact location, ordered us to pull back, hopefully out of sight of the German mortar observers. Shortly after we started moving back, the mortar fire started up again. There weren't any holes to get into there, so most of the men in my platoon jumped into a huge crater caused by the explosion of a large artillery shell. The way they were lying in the crater reminded me of grade school in the winter back in Minnesota when a boy would fall down at the end of an icy slide, and all the other boys would jump on top of him yelling, "Hog pile!"

I can still recall the men lying face down, with arms and legs extended in spread eagle positions, some at the bottom of the crater and others lying on top of them. Bonnet was among those on the top tier of bodies. One shell could have killed them all. The entire company halted, and many of the men, including myself, could find no cover. The German mortar fire was not so heavy as it had been in the previous barrage, but if we stayed where we were, we were sure to suffer heavy casualties. There was a feeling of helplessness like being caught out in an open field with no place to hide. I located Chambers and said, "Sir, we better get out of here as quick as possible. The way we're bunched up without cover, we'll be in real trouble if they start up again."

"Okay, Devitt," he said. "Ya'll lead us out and I'll catch up in a couple minutes."

I called to my men in the crater, and they and the rest of the company followed me out of the area. Soon Chambers caught up and led the company to the place where we were to stay for the night.

The area was still heavily wooded. But just beyond us, toward the Germans, there was an open field that dropped down into a valley and then, beyond, there were more trees. The field was about a half mile across. While looking at this panorama, we saw an American tank come out of the trees at the far side of the field. It seemed to be going at top speed. From the trees, a German antitank gun began to fire. It hit the tank, which then stopped. I can't remember the crew getting out of the tank, but perhaps they did. We did not go down to the tank to investigate or attempt a rescue. It would not have been worth risking the lives of several of our men in order to try to rescue four or five tankers who might already have been killed or captured.

Soon after, the winter night started to set in. I usually shared my foxhole with Elliott, my radioman. He came to me and said, "Lieutenant, would you mind if I spend the night with Holmgren and Rosenthal.[9] They've got a big hole with plenty of logs on top."

"That's better than I'll have," I said, "but we both've had better places to sleep before. Go ahead and stay with them, but report back to me first thing in the morning."

"Thanks, Lieutenant. I'll see you in the morning."

During the night the German artillery came in heavily on our positions. The trees were not so thick as in some other places, so the tree bursts were not so frequent. In the morning, I got out of my hole and asked for Elliott. I was told that a direct hit had killed everyone in his hole. I was stunned and shocked, but not terribly surprised. This might sound blasé, but death was part of our life. I wish now that I had written to Elliott's parents about their son's death, especially since I later learned that he was an only child. I suppose that I had seen so much death that writing to someone's parents did not occur to me at the time.

I didn't write any letters during the entire time I was in the Hürtgen. I don't think that I carried any writing paper and besides, I might have been hauled off by the men in white coats if anyone had seen a crazy lieutenant trying to write a letter in

---

[9]These are not the actual names of the two men with whom Elliott shared the hole. I simply don't recall their names.

the cold and wet and mud and filth and death and destruction of the forest.

That evening two of the men were digging a foxhole and saw that some big rocks in the ground prevented them from going deep enough, so they decided to find another site. It was almost pitch black by this time, and luckily they found a near-by slit trench that they thought was a good start for a decent hole. All they had to do was widen it a foot or so and perhaps deepen it a little, and then there would be enough room for both. One of them jumped into the hole and started to dig. With the first shovelful, he caught the foul odor of human excrement. They had chosen for their foxhole the site of a German army latrine.

Attack toward Strass

In the morning we advanced through the woods toward Strass, a small town located in a treeless area two or three hundred yards east of the edge of the woods. There was more forest several hundred yards east of Strass. From the edge of the woods, the ground dropped gradually into Strass. From the height at the edge of the woods one could see a vast area of lower ground stretching to the Roer River including the towns of Gey and Strass and the wooded areas beyond them. The Third Battalion of the 330th had spent the last three days battling the Germans to get into Strass and then fighting to dislodge them from the town. The Third Battalion was finally successful in driving the Germans out of Strass, but the Germans merely retreated to the forest to the east. From there, they were able to observe the men of the Third Battalion and continue to pour devastating fire upon them. The Third Battalion was stuck out in the open like ducks on a pond, and the Germans were the successful hunters. All of this resulted in the Third Battalion losing half of its men, so they were in no condition to continue the fight. The Second Battalion was, therefore, ordered to advance into Strass to relieve the Third and then continue the attack eastward past Strass.

As our leading scouts reached the edge of the woods and cautiously advanced into the open toward Strass, the Germans started to fire their fearsome 88s at us. All of us immediately scrambled back to find cover in the woods, knowing that if we just stood around unprotected, we would not be long for this world. The 88 was a multipurpose 88-millimeter artillery piece used against tanks and infantry as well as in the anti-aircraft role for which it had been designed. It was a long-barreled gun with a high muzzle velocity, so when it fired, the shell reached its target quickly. It was also very accurate. From the time of their first shots, they were right on target.

Fortunately, there were a few dugouts, which the Germans had built, and into which some of the men were able to find cover. The dugouts were probably six feet deep, with a heavy layer of logs covering the top. They were deep enough for a man to stand and large enough to sleep six to ten men. In contrast, the foxholes were two or three feet deep, about the same width, and long enough that a man could stretch out, but only large enough for two or three men. Those of us who did not have a dugout were obliged to find a dip in the ground or to dig a hole as quickly as possible. I was in this latter group. The shelling was especially frightening since we knew that the Germans could see where we were, and were able to fire directly at our positions with their 88s.

Talmer Brill was a staff sergeant from Virginia who had been a squad leader and also platoon guide in the third platoon. He was about six feet three inches tall and built like a heavyweight champion. His size and commanding presence assured that his men followed his orders without hesitation.

Brill and I were lying in a ditch near each other while the 88 (and other artillery) shells were coming in. At such a time, although someone may be close to you, there is a feeling of fear, loneliness, and helplessness, as though there is nothing that can prevent you from being killed under the unrelenting crashing of shells.

While we lay there, we talked of how cold we were getting.

"Brill," I said, "I'm gettin' awful cold."

"Lieutenant," he replied, "I could sure use an overcoat."

If I had been in a jocular frame of mind, I might have said, "Don't worry, Brill. The Army always takes care of us. I'll bet we'll have overcoats by summer."

I don't recall how I answered Brill, but it was probably something cryptic and unimaginative such as, "Me, too."

We wore field jackets, woolen sweaters, woolen shirts and trousers, cotton fatigue shirts and trousers, and long winter underwear, together with one or two pairs of heavy socks and high top leather shoes, as well as woolen gloves and a woolen cap topped off by the steel helmet on our heads.

If we could have been granted one wish at the time, I'm sure that both Brill and I (rather than overcoats) would have wished to leave that killing ground. It was not the cold that was getting to us, but the 88s. Yet for us, as leaders, to leave and to go to the rear without a compelling reason would have been unthinkable. Aside from the possibility of a court martial for desertion, such behavior would have been demoralizing to the rest of the men, and would have been an invitation for others to follow.

Something causes men who are threatened with imminent death or injury to stay in their positions and not flee. That something is discipline. It encompasses a number of things, such as training, respect for authority, pride in doing one's duty, esprit de corps, fear of failure, peer pressure, and following the example of leaders. Although Brill and I were scared to death and wanted to leave, discipline kept us where we were. But if Brill and I had gone to the rear, there could have been a breakdown of discipline and the entire company might have fled.

Futch and Kurek

Futch was a young, round-faced Southern boy who was very religious. Before we entered combat, evenings were often spent sitting around a campfire talking, and whenever one of the men used profanity, Futch would stop him and remind him

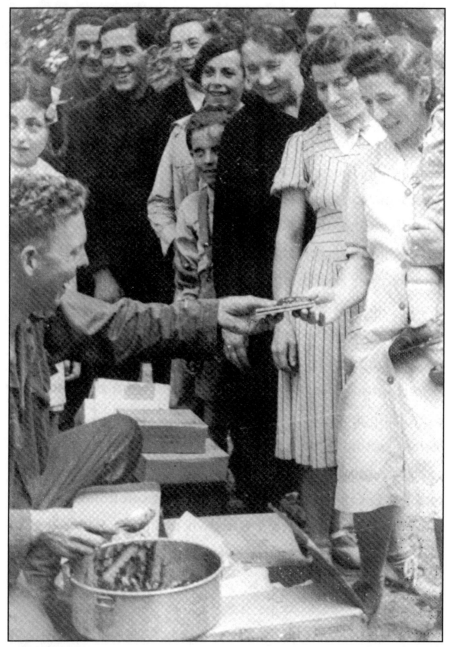

Talmer Brill in Luxembourg. I'm not sure that this was Brill, but if it wasn't, it was his identical twin, if he had one. I don't know what they were doing, but, clearly, it was a happy occasion. (Courtesy of the 83rd Infantry Division Association)

not to use such language. He'd say earnestly, "Hey, fella, that's no way to talk. What would your mama say if she heard ya?"

The men respected him, and I think they watched their language when he was nearby. He was only nineteen or twenty years old, but he was married and had one or two children.

Sometime after I had talked to Brill, I discovered that Futch and another man, Kurek, were not with the rest of us. They were buddies, although they were very different from each other. Futch was a Southerner while Kurek was from the Northeast. Futch was against drinking and swearing while I think that Kurek was like the other men in that respect. They might have been called the "odd couple," but they were inseparable. As soon as the fire from the 88s let up, I ran back to find them.

On the way back I was running through a small clearing in the trees when a couple shots were fired just over my head.

I immediately hit the ground, and since I was in the open and didn't know where the fire was coming from, I raised my arms in surrender. Much to my dismay, there was no German soldier to accept my surrender. I sheepishly lowered my arms. I didn't know where the firing came from, but I'm sure that I didn't later tell my men of my unbecoming behavior.

I soon found Futch and Kurek a short distance behind the rest of the company. Apparently they were at the rear of the company when the 88s first fired on us, and they stayed where they were.

I told them to follow me to the forward position. I started out running full speed with Futch behind me by about ten yards and Kurek following Futch. Infantry tactics call for men to keep spread out and not to bunch up. The reason, obviously, is that the further apart the men are, the less chance a single round of artillery (or burst of small arms fire) will hit them all. As we ran forward, I heard an artillery shell coming in. I hit the ground, and at the same time the shell landed behind me with a deafening explosion. It fell no more than ten yards away. Dirt and shrapnel sailed through the air, and although I was peppered with chunks of dirt, the shrapnel flew over me, and I was untouched. The concussion from the exploding shell shook me like the vibration from a passing freight train, but somehow I was still alive. I looked back and saw the black smoke from the shell. The acrid vapor stung my eyes. It appeared as though a dense dark cloud had suddenly descended upon us.

I got up and walked back into the smoke. I heard Kurek yelling, "Futch, Futch!" As the smoke cleared a little, I looked down and saw Futch lying motionless on the ground face up. He was dead. Half of his head and face had been torn away by the shell. His head looked as though a sharp ax had cleanly through it. I still remember looking down at his brains, which were laid bare from the blast. It has been over fifty years since this happened, and the memory of Futch's death is still as clear as the day it happened. I cannot forget it.

I could do nothing for Futch, so I went back to Kurek, who had been hit in several places on his body, including wounds in his arms and legs. He was also bleeding from his head. He was crying hysterically, "Futch, Futch, help me! Help me!"

"Settle down, Kurek. You'll be all right," I said. "Here, I'll help ya into that dugout."

"Lieutenant, help me!"

"Okay. Okay."

I dragged him over to a nearby dugout and put him down into it.

"Take it easy," I said. "I don't know if you could see him, but Futch didn't make it."

Kurek quieted down a little and said, "That's what I figured. It must have hit him square. He was right in the middle." Then he started up again, "Lieutenant, help me. Get me out of here. Don't go! Please!"

"Don't worry," I said. "I'll get help right away. I'll have someone back here in five minutes. We'll get a litter, and you'll be away from this mess real soon. I don't blame ya for being scared, but you'll be okay. I'm scared too. By tonight you'll be safe and warm, and we'll still be here. Try to think ahead to tonight. You're going to make it."

"Lieutenant, please don't leave me. Please don't go."

He was afraid of dying alone in that dark German hole.

"Kurek, I've got to get back to the company. I promise ya, I'll send a medic right away. So long."

"Lieutenant, please don't leave me. Please! Please!"

I just couldn't stay with him; he needed more help than I could give. My place was with my other men. I left him and ran forward to the rest of the company. When I got there, I sent a medic back to him. I neither saw nor heard from Kurek again, but I learned later that he survived.

What happened to Futch and Kurek must have been repeated, with variations, thousands of times during the war. Two obscure young infantrymen, without hesitation, followed the order of their lieutenant and ran directly into death and serious injury. No one was there to applaud or say, "Well done, soldier!" If they had been struck down while overwhelming an enemy stronghold, they might have been recognized for their bravery and steadfastness. But no, one was killed and one was mutilated under the same circumstances that many infantry casualties found themselves—alone and barely noticed. Of course I was there. But I didn't even think of saying a prayer for Futch, nor did I soften up enough to try to give Kurek a little more comfort from his fear and pain. God knows why I didn't, but I don't. I wish that there were some way I could easily describe what they, as front-line infantrymen, went through. Many people think that all soldiers' experiences are much alike. But that isn't true. The front-line infantryman comprised about one out of five soldiers. That twenty percent probably suffered ninety percent of the casualties. He was involved in a risky business. The front-line infantryman, just for being and staying in combat, deserves the admiration, praise, and thanks of all his countrymen.

At the time I hit the ground to avoid the shell that killed Futch, my helmet fell off, but I didn't notice it because of the exploding shell and heavy smoke. A helmet had the tendency

Medics tending to a wounded man in a Hürtgen town, fall 1944. (Photo courtesy of 83rd Infantry Division Association)

to fall off because we fastened its chin strap around the back of the helmet rather than under the chin where it would keep the helmet from falling off. The reason we did this is because we were told that if we had the chin strap under the chin, the concussion from the explosion of a nearby shell could drive the helmet upward together with the chin strap (and the chin) resulting in a broken neck. Until now I had not recognized that I might have died or been paralyzed if my chin strap had been in place.

After returning to the company, I realized that the helmet was missing, but I was not going to wander around looking for a helmet while the 88s were zeroed in on us. Bonnet had just been wounded by the artillery fire and was being evacuated. I felt very vulnerable without a helmet, so I said to him, "Bonnet, I lost my helmet when I hit the ground back there. Would you mind if I took yours?"

"Lieutenant, I've had this helmet ever since we landed in Normandy, and you know with these two holes in it, I'd hate to give it up. If I ever get home, it'll be proof I was here."

He kept the helmet. I didn't blame him.

We stayed in the woods all day waiting for nightfall before going down into Strass. During the day, Colonel Foster, the regimental commander, came up to E Company, probably to see if we could move ahead faster. After he had been there for a while, he no longer had to worry about how fast we moved. The colonel got hit by a piece of shrapnel. It was not a serious wound, but it sliced the skin just below the chin. A wound like that would have made most of us happy, because we would have been evacuated away from the combat zone. But Colonel Foster, who was a regular (career) army officer, probably stayed out of combat for as short a time as possible. The career officer's future advancement depended on his performance in combat, so he had more incentive than the rest of us to remain in combat as long as possible.

About the same time as Colonel Foster was hit, Frank Chambers was also wounded. Before going into the army, he had been a professional baseball player, having played part of a season (just before the army got him) with the old Washington Senators (now the Minnesota Twins). He was hit by shrapnel in the upper part of his right arm—his throwing arm. I often wondered if the wound affected his baseball career after the war. I looked in the baseball box scores after I got home, but I never did see Chambers' name in any lineup. Again, I neither saw nor heard of him after he was wounded.

Strass

As soon as it got dark enough, we left the woods and walked down the hill to Strass. It was a small town of no more than 100 buildings with a long main street running north and south and on which most of the buildings were located. We proceeded single file to avoid land mines and so that no one would get lost. There was no problem with the men staying in line directly behind each other, for we all knew that to step out of line could have brought immediate death from a mine. The engineers had cleared a path with mine detectors and marked it so we knew where to go.

The battalion commander, Colonel Norris, was with us, since the Second Battalion was relieving the Third.

The Germans had a cute little anti-personnel mine to which some homesick American soldier attached a name that might have been given to a childhood toy. It was called a Bouncing Betty. The ingenious feature of the Bouncing Betty was that instead of exploding on the ground when it was tripped off, it would spring up into the air to about the height of a man and then explode and hurl its dozens of ball-bearing pellets or shrapnel pieces in all directions, so that instead of getting only one man with a single explosion, Bouncing Betty could get ten at time.

I don't know what the Germans called it. I'm sure that if they had a name for it, the name would not have been as simple as Bouncing Betty because of the German penchant for attaching to something a name that described it in precise detail. They often combined several words to make up a new

An after-battle view of Strass, showing the Hürtgen Forest in the background. The forest was located on the high ground west of the town. On the evening of December 12, 1944, E Company walked out of the forest down into Strass. (Photo courtesy of the 83rd Infantry Division Association)

and much longer word. For example, the Main Office of Reich Security was a single word, *Reichssicherheitshauptamt.*

The German name for a Bouncing Betty might have been in German in the form of one long word showing the German propensity for detail, "The anti-personnelminethatleapsintotheairtotheheightofaman(between25.5centemetersand-30.3centimeters)explodingandhurtlingitspellets(.10centemeterindiameter)inalldirections-M3."

After we got into Strass, I was walking with Colonel Norris, when I tripped and fell to the ground. At the same time, a German shell exploded but not very close to us. Colonel Norris looked down at me and said, "Are you hit?"

I got up and said, "No, sir, I just tripped."

I felt sort of ashamed, feeling that the colonel might have thought that I was hitting the ground as a reaction to a shell that landed so far away that I would not have been hit. I was afraid that the colonel would think less of me because of this. But I'm sure that the colonel as well as I had more important things to worry about.

The Third platoon spent the night in the basement of an abandoned house, for the townspeople had already fled. When we got into the house, we received food for the evening. This consisted of three boxes of K rations for the whole platoon, which I estimate (considering the casualties of the last two weeks) numbered fifteen to twenty men out of the original forty. This is the only time while I was with E Company that we ever failed to get a full ration of food. Of course, the food wasn't always quite like mother used to make.

Some time before E Company entered the Hürtgen Forest, Lieutenant Robert Packer arrived. He was made commander of the weapons platoon because the lieutenant who had that job in France and Luxembourg before we entered the Hürtgen had hurt his leg and could not stay with the company. Packer was a good-looking, apple-cheeked fellow, who was probably a year or two older than I, making him twenty-two or twenty-three years of age. He was from the northeast. I think Rhode Island. I had the impression that he was from a fairly well-to-do family, since his father owned some kind of business. On occasion he would read excerpts from letters from his father. Except for this, I knew nothing of his background. I learned that he had been in E Company before I joined it, and had been hospitalized before returning to the company prior to the Hürtgen campaign.

A Battle Outside of the Bulge

After Chambers was wounded, the executive officer, Berry, became the company commander. He was a blonde fellow from the Chicago area, about twenty-five years of age. He and I entered combat at the same time.

Early in the morning following our entry into Strass, we received orders to attack the Germans who were in a woods about 600 yards east of the town. For those unfamiliar with it, one principle in infantry tactics is the line of departure, which is the line from which the attack begins. If the attack is to begin at, say, 7:00 A.M., the forward elements of the attacking unit cross the line of departure at that time. It is always well within the lines of the attacking force.

East of Strass was a two-story, brick house, which stood alone, 200 yards from the nearest building in town. Near the house were two American Sherman tanks. Four hundred yards farther to the east, beyond the brick house, was the edge of the woods, where the Germans were located. We were to commence the attack just before daylight, so that we could cross the 600 yards of open ground before the Germans could see us. The line of departure was an imaginary line running through the brick house. Our plan was to pass to the left of the house and to proceed straight east to the woods. (See map on page 112.)

The land across which we were to advance was as flat as a parade ground with few ditches or gullies to slide into in order to avoid incoming fire. Wartime vegetable gardens probably had occupied the space during the summer and fall. The December weather reminded me of a crisp November day in Minnesota. The temperature was about freezing so that if pre-

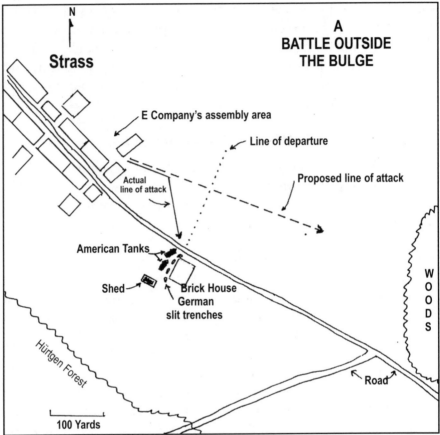

cipitation would have come, it would have been snow rather than rain.

In an attack, the usual procedure was for our artillery or mortars or both to support the attacking force by shelling the enemy position. But in this one, we had no such support because we were to start before daylight and did not want to alert the German defenders so that we could get across the open field before they knew we were coming. We intended this to be a surprise assault against them, but, unfortunately for us, it turned out to be more of a surprise to us than to them.

We started out walking in two parallel columns about twenty yards apart. Our plan was that when we would get close to the enemy position, or if we were fired on before that, we would form a skirmish line and continue the attack. We planned to go well to the left (north) of the house and to proceed east to the edge of the woods where the enemy awaited us. The pace was rather slow since we had to walk carefully in order to make as little noise as possible. We also had the constant danger of walking into a mine field.

The left column was the first platoon and the right column, the third. The second platoon was in the rear as the reserve. Instead of the normal strength of forty men, each platoon was down to fifteen to twenty men. The company commander was toward the rear of the left column. As leader of the third platoon, I was in the middle of the right column.

Even though the night was dark, we could see the outlines of the brick house and the American tanks. After we had advanced about half way to the house, small arms fire started to come at us from in and around the house. There was also machine gun fire from the tanks. We all hit the ground. To say that we were surprised would be a major understatement. American tanks should have American soldiers in them. Instead, machine gun fire was coming from them. The Germans had somehow captured the tanks and had turned our machine guns against us. Military theory told us that the line of departure (near where the tanks were located) should have been well within our lines. But instead we were being fired upon by the Germans from positions within our lines—or, which we thought were. We were having to fight to reach the line of departure.

As soon as they hit the ground, many of the men started to fire back. There was plenty of fire power on both sides. Apart from the M-1 rifles, we had five or six BARs (Browning automatic rifles), two light machine guns, and a few Tommy guns (Thompson sub-machine guns). Besides the two .50-caliber machine guns on the American tanks, the Germans had their own machine guns, burp guns (machine pistols) and bolt action rifles. We out-gunned them, but not by much, and we had to get off the ground and run across 100 yards of open field. With all those weapons, bullets soon filled the air from both directions.

Many men returned the fire, but not I. When I hit the ground I first tried to get lower than the surface. Machine gun fire was going right over my head, and I would have been much more comfortable if I had been a foot or two lower. Death was nearby. The crack, crack of bullets close to my head told me to keep my head down. Those not so close made a swishing sound, and fortunately for me there were more swishers than crackers. The trick was to get your head up when enemy fire was not being directed toward you in order to observe, or to fire, or to advance.

I tried to think of what to do. In order for an attacker to advance against a defender who is firing, the attacker must attain fire superiority—something I first learned about at St. Thomas. This means that the attacker must direct a large enough volume of fire against the defender to slow or halt the firing of the defender. Tied in with fire superiority is the concept of fire and movement—meaning that while some of the attackers are firing and gaining fire superiority, others are moving forward.

After a few minutes of furious exchange of fire between us and the Germans, their fire let up noticeably. Fire superiority? I don't know, but before I could decide what orders to give or even to fire a shot, one of our men got up and ran forward.

He was immediately followed by others. The rest of the company then rose and ran toward the brick house. A few men might have fired from the hip while advancing, but most of us, including myself, just ran as fast as we could to cover the open ground as quickly as possible. I don't know who gave the orders or who was the first to move forward. I do know that it was not I, and I am not proud of this.

I had pretty good reasons for failing to lead the attack, namely, I was frightened and also pinned down by machine gun fire snapping over my head. The only reason that occurs to me as to why others were able to commence firing and move forward before I was able to, is that the incoming fire was not so close to them as it was to me. Of course they might have had stiffer stuff in their spines. In other words, they probably had more courage than I. But Uncle Sam was not paying me $125 a month to wait for someone else to do the job. I should have made an estimate of the situation, decided what to do, and then done it.

Quite suddenly the deep dark of night began to disappear, and dim daylight was rapidly approaching.

Off to the right of the house was a wooden shed. Many of the German soldiers had gone back into the house, but some remained in slit trenches in front of it. As I approached the house and came near one of the tanks, I stopped running and began to walk forward cautiously with the butt of my M-1 tucked into my shoulder ready to fire my first shot in combat. How could this be my first shot in combat since we had been fighting the Germans for the last ten days? In my very limited combat experience, I hadn't had the opportunity to shoot. As a leader, my job was not so much to do the firing myself, but to direct the actions of my men.

Out of the dark ground and into the dim light a German soldier leaped out of a slit trench directly in front of me. He was facing the shed with his back to me. He raised his arms in surrender. Before I could do or say anything, one of my men, Red Robinson, came around the shed, face to face with the German and shot him dead as I looked on. I was stunned. I recognized immediately that if Red's bullets had missed the man, they would have hit me. I was about to accept the surrender of a German soldier who was no more than five feet ahead of me only to have him fall dead at my feet.

In retrospect, I could have turned Red in for shooting a man who was surrendering. But we were busy with other things at the time. The Germans were still firing at us, and we had not yet reached the line of departure. Besides, I wasn't certain that Red had seen the German raise his hands before Red fired. Further, if someone is trying to shoot you, do hostilities cease as soon as he drops his gun and raises his arms? One minute Red was being subjected to enemy fire. The next, he had to stop and decide to be kind and forgiving—and, more difficult, unafraid. That might be too much to ask of anyone.

I'm sure that philosophers can write pages on what the proper conduct for both Red and me should have been. And the philosophers can speak with certainty and conviction as to the right action to take. But they weren't there, and I was. And I'm not so certain.

We later learned that a few days earlier the American tanks had advanced as far as the brick house and that they had been knocked out by German bazookas or *Panzerfausts*. I don't know what happened to the tank crews or the infantrymen, if any, who accompanied them.

The company now had the brick house surrounded. The Germans were inside, and ungraciously did not want us to share the building with them. Their fire had subsided considerably from what it had been. Since we had recaptured the two American tanks, all that was left was sporadic fire from rifles and burp guns coming from the building's windows. It seemed that the German vocabulary did not include the word "surrender."

Several of my men and I were behind one of the two American tanks, shielded from the building and the German fire. Sergeant Ralph White, who had become platoon sergeant after Bonnet was wounded a few days earlier, saw that we needed to get inside the house quickly. The tank we were behind was only five or ten yards from the house. Its machine gun, was on top of the tank next to the hatch on the tank's turret. He said, "Lieutenant, do you think that machine gun's working?"

"I don't know," I replied. "Are you going to try it?"

"Yeah. Gimme a boost up."

He put one foot on the tank's tread, and I pushed him up. He crawled over to the machine gun, cocked it, and then sprayed the windows and the side of the building with the powerful .50-caliber bullets. They shattered the windows and ripped the side of the building, throwing chunks of brick everywhere.

Moments later from an upstairs window, the Germans responded predictably. A long handled "potato masher" grenade came tumbling through the air. It landed on the tank and exploded in front of White.

He was hit and fell backwards unconscious off the tank into my arms. His helmet dropped to the ground, and blood was pouring down his head and face and from his hands, and it started to ooze through his field jacket.

Fortunately one of our medics had been able to stick near us, and he took over immediately. I could see that White was hurt badly, but I didn't know the extent of his injuries, nor did I have time to stand around and watch. My job was to stop the enemy fire and get into the house. I never again saw White, although I later learned that he survived.

When the grenade exploded, I felt a sting on my right temple. A tiny piece of shrapnel had somehow slipped past White and hit me. It was the slightest of wounds, and I didn't think about it. If the German grenade had been thrown too hard it might have landed past White and fallen off the tank and exploded at my feet. If that had happened, instead of White, several of us on the ground would have been killed or wounded.

Our men immediately emulated White and poured small arms fire through the windows. The only response from the Germans was some rifle fire and an occasional brief flurry from a burp gun. The German soldier would raise his head above the window sill and fire a burst or two and then quickly duck down. Although it was getting light out, he had not the time, nor undoubtedly the inclination, to find and aim at the American infantrymen. One or two of the Germans might have been hit by our fire before they could have got back down.

After the war, I submitted a recommendation that White be awarded the Silver Star for gallantry in action. I don't know whether or not he received the medal, although, in my opinion, his actions warranted a half dozen of them. He risked his life, and almost lost it, by his unhesitating courage in scrambling up the tank and firing the machine gun at point blank range. He, thereby, invited the almost certain response from the enemy of exploding a grenade next to him, resulting in the unnumbered and nearly deadly shrapnel wounds to his body.

We still weren't in the house, for the stubborn Germans would not surrender. (If they had been American, I would surely have called them "brave.")

I told one of my men with a grenade adapter on the end of his rifle to follow me. A rifle grenade was attached to the adapter, and the rifle would be fired toward the target launching the grenade. My plan was to fire a grenade into an upstairs window driving the surviving Germans to the ground floor.

"Fire a grenade through that window," I said to my grenade launcher man. But before he could fire, I said, "Wait, try the window to the right. Just a second, let's try the window on the other side."

I couldn't decide into which window to fire. My indecisiveness reminds me of the old sailor in the A.A. Milne poem[10] who was shipwrecked on an island. As he was lying on the beach, he couldn't decide what he should do first. He thought he would begin by looking for a spring (for water), but changed his mind and decided to build a hut, and hesitated again and thought he would make a large sun-stopping hat. Since he couldn't decide what to do first, he did nothing at all

---

[10]Entitled "The Old Sailor," in A. A. Milne's book, *Now We Are Six*.

and lay on the beach until he was rescued. Unlike the old sailor I had decided what to do, but, before I could to it, someone else fired a rifle grenade into an upstairs window forcing the Germans to flee down to the ground floor.

We threw hand grenades into the lower windows and prepared to rush in through the front door. Just then, the Germans started to come out the door, with their arms raised in surrender. There were about twenty of them.

As we lined up the prisoners to lead them to the rear, one of the prisoners, an officer, acted in a haughty manner and was slow, even reluctant, to get into line. Our friend Red did not take such reluctance lightly. He walked up to the German officer and kicked him in the seat of the pants to move him along. I suppose there is some rule of war that proscribes kicking enemy officers in the seat of the pants, but I felt like cheering.

It's hard to make even a close guess as to the number of casualties we and the Germans suffered. We won the skirmish, so one might conclude that the losers had more casualties. But I think the opposite might have been true since we were the attackers and had to run forward in the open through enemy fire without the protection of foxholes or other cover. I estimate that each side suffered at least twenty to twenty-five killed and wounded. In addition, we took about twenty prisoners.

At the beginning of the attack, our company had a total of about ninety men. Ten of these were part of the company's support personnel, that is, the mess sergeant, cooks, the supply sergeant and his assistants, and the two jeep drivers. That left eighty men to participate in the attack. Of that eighty, there were the fifteen men of the sixty-millimeter mortar section who were back in Strass manning the three mortars. That left about sixty-five men from E Company who advanced in the attack against the brick house. At the end of the day, that group was reduced to about forty. That means that we went down from sixty-five to forty men in less than an hour.

An observer might think that Americans were the victors since we defeated the Germans by taking the brick house.

On the other hand, one or two more victories like that and E Company would have been out of business. We would have run out of bodies to continue the fight.

Berry was hit during the attack, so Packer became company commander. Although Berry commanded the company for only a few days, he nevertheless distinguished himself. He led the company in the attack on the brick house and was wounded while leading his men.

Packer and I were the only officers left in the company. I don't know if he just took over command because he outranked me, or whether Colonel Norris radioed to Packer to assume command. I know that I had no doubts that he should be company commander, because he was a first lieutenant and I a second.

As soon as the prisoners were sent to the rear, all of the men in the company went into the basement of the house, for that was the safest place around. We did not even try to advance further that day across the open field to the forest beyond. We were stuck out in front of the rest of the American lines, unable to advance or retreat. Since we had planned to cross the open field leading to the Germans in the woods before daylight and had no idea we would have to fight for the brick house and lose about a fourth of the company in doing so, we did not even consider continuing the attack that day. The basement consisted of two large rooms. The walls and ceiling were made of brick or concrete. It was built like a bunker.

There were about forty men in the basement. The rest of the company, about twenty to thirty, did not get to the brick house, and ended up back in Strass.

When we first got down to the basement, a dead German soldier lay sprawled on the floor. One of the men in the company prided himself on the number of watches he had taken from prisoners. He had about ten German watches. He and I came upon the dead German at the same time. Our "watch man" immediately reached down and took one from the dead man's wrist. He looked at me triumphantly, as though he had beaten me in a contest. I thought for a moment, and then pushed back with my foot the sleeve on the dead man's other wrist. As I had hoped, the other wrist also held a watch. I said quietly, "Please give me *that* watch." I felt that I had won! I can't explain such ghoulish behavior. Perhaps, after seeing so much death, one becomes blasé and does not view death with the awe that usually accompanies it.

After the company had gathered in the basement of the building and the shooting had stopped, we at last felt safe and secure. Although we were an obvious target for the Germans in the woods, there was nevertheless a feeling of peacefulness after the firefight. One of the men went up the basement stairs and outside of the house. As soon as he stepped outside, fire came from the German-held woods. He was killed immediately. So much for our feeling of security.

While in the basement, the first sergeant noticed that I was bleeding from my right temple. He said to me, "What happened to your head, Lieutenant?"

"Oh, that. It's nothing. I got nicked by the grenade that got White. I was lucky."

"Well, I'll put it on the morning report. I suppose you'll get a Purple Heart."

"Oh, I don't know. I don't think so."

He noted my wound in the morning report, and I later received a Purple Heart for this slight wound. It was about one inch from my right eye. Another inch to the left and the little piece of shrapnel would have hit my eye and possibly blinded me. I had not considered such a possibility until writing this, so I'm more moved by the incident now than I was when it happened.

The wound did me much more good than harm. After the war in Europe ended, there was a point system by which the men having more points would be sent home first. They were given for battle stars, decorations, and time overseas. Since the Purple Heart was worth five points, it helped me get home at an earlier date.

Soon after the man went up the basement stairs and was killed outside of the house, white phosphorous shells began to fall near the house. When a white phosphorous round explodes, it throws burning phosphorous in all directions, forming a cloud of white smoke and burning whatever it contacts. There wasn't anything to do but hope and pray that the house would not be hit and catch fire. Out of a basement window we saw a man running toward us, coming from the south. When he got to us, we saw that he was an American lieutenant from the Fifth Armored Division, which was attacking south of us. He looked dirty and disheveled and was breathless, for he had just sprinted several hundred yards to reach us. He did not know whether the brick house was occupied by Germans or Americans, since our attack took place largely in the dark. His unit had fired the white phosphorous trying to smoke us out and find out who we were. When we did not come out of the building, he decided to see for himself, and he risked his life running hundreds of yards in the open to reach us. He at least stopped the mortar fire that had us worried. Here again was another unsung hero who, I presume, didn't get recognized for his bravery.

When he got to us in the basement, Packer said to him, "I'm Bob Packer, E Company, 330th. What's up, Lieutenant?"

"I'm from the Fifth Armored," he replied. "We're in those woods," he said, nodding to the south, "and we didn't know if you were Germans or Americans. We knew you were in Strass, but didn't know if you'd got past it to this house. We knew something was going on from all the firing, but we couldn't tell who held the house because it was so dark. We didn't want to advance out of the woods if the Germans were here and could deliver flanking fire on us. So I decided to find out, and here I am."

"You did a good job getting here. I hope you can get back. We can't advance out of here in the daylight, but I expect we'll try to get into those woods to the east tomorrow morning. We don't have any hot chow, but here's a K ration if you're hungry."

"No thanks. We've got plenty of chow in our tanks. I'd better get back." And off he went.

As the night came on and we began to think of where to sleep, Packer said to me, "Bill, I think we should sleep in separate rooms. If a shell hits this house, I want to be sure it won't get us both, so you go in there."

His concern was that, since the company was down to only two officers, there should be one officer to lead the company if the house were hit. I went into the other room in the basement. The floor was already completely covered with men trying to sleep. I returned and said, "That room is more packed than this. Of course I could sleep outdoors if you'd like," I added slyly.

"Say, wise guy," he said, "I should take you up on that. Okay, stay here."

I guess that Packer was too tired to argue, so I stayed in the room where he was. I didn't care where I slept. It did not change my chances of being killed or wounded. I, therefore, felt that the war effort would not be diminished substantially if Lieutenants Packer and Devitt should simultaneously be relieved of their duties by enemy fire.

Someone might ask why we attacked without knowing whether or not the Germans were in the brick house. And why was the line of departure set near the brick house 200 yards beyond the town from which the company started?

I don't know, but I'll speculate. The first thing to consider is the nature of infantry fighting. In theory, the company commander gives a detailed attack order to the platoon leaders, and they, in turn, pass it on to the squad leaders who then tell their men. After the attack begins, the company commander advises the reserve platoon to reinforce one of the lead platoons that has met heavy resistance.

That all sounds logical and fine on paper, but, in my experience, it seldom worked out that way. We have all played the game "telephone" in which a person whispers a short message to someone next to him, and the message is then repeated from person to person around a circle. The result is that the last person to get the message seldom understands the same message that the first person actually gave. I suspect that by the time the company commander's order reached the privates in the platoons, there was some garbling of the order.

The company commander, Berry, was wounded during our attack, so there was a switch in command. One of the two remaining officers, Packer, took over while we were in the middle of the attack in the black of night and being fired on by an enemy from a nearby location, which we thought was held by our own men. The company commander, who was running the show, was stopped by a German bullet and lost to us. Would that add to the confusion? I think so.

An infantry assault is not an exact science. Rather, in my opinion, in many instances it can best be described as mass confusion. Men are often firing at targets they can't see and are moving toward an enemy whose location is uncertain. The human element makes everything so unpredictable that sometimes the best a commander can do is to point his men in the right direction, send them off, and hope for the best. That seems cynical, but I think it is closer to the truth than some tacticians might acknowledge.

Why would we attack without first determining who was in the brick house? Keep in mind that the Second Battalion (including our company) had entered Strass in the dark the evening before the attack, and our company was ordered to begin the attack before daylight of the following morning. Although both our battalion and company commanders probably observed the brick house, they also saw the two American tanks behind the house, away from the Germans in the woods (where we believed the Germans were dug in). This probably seemed to the two commanders to be the natural position for the American tanks to be in to avoid enemy fire. They, therefore, would have assumed that there were Americans in the American tanks. The men from our Third Battalion, who had taken Strass, perhaps were not aware that the tanks had been knocked out by the Germans. If they were aware, then they somehow forgot to tell our battalion and company commanders. Again, the human element?

How can I explain why the line of departure was set by the company commander near the brick house, 200 yards beyond the town? The company commander's thinking might have been something like this. "There are Americans in the brick house. That must be our most advanced position so the line of departure should be up there. We shouldn't start an attack from behind our own lines. If we start the attack from back here in Strass and if our unit in the brick house has an outpost or two dug into the ground we're attacking over, we might mistake them for the enemy and fire at them. I'll set the line of departure out near to the brick house, so the attack won't begin until we get up there."

I don't know that we would have done things differently if we had known that the Germans were in the brick house. If we'd sent a patrol to see who was there, this could have alerted the Germans, and they might have started firing at us even earlier than they did. All of this just seems to corroborate my impression of infantry fighting in which each individual soldier seems to be fighting his own personal war. He concentrates on a single enemy or objective and fights doggedly to win. Thus the battle is a series of little battles fought simultaneously in which the combatants tend to muddle along until one side or the other may be able to declare that it is the victor.

Attack Past the Brick House

Early the next morning we attacked toward the woods to the east, the same woods which was our original objective the morning before when we were diverted by fire from the brick house.

We planned the attack to be similar to that of the previous day. We set off before daylight in two columns with the hope of reaching the woods before the enemy spotted us. Fortunately, the sky was overcast so there was no moonlight. There were only about forty men left in the three rifle platoons, so we consolidated the three into one, and I was the leader. Packer was immediately to the rear of the two columns, and I was in the middle of the right one. Instead of 600 yards of open ground to cross as we had the day before, we had "only" 400 yards to the edge of the woods.

Since the Germans had fired at us from the woods after we had taken the brick house, we knew for certain that they were there and waiting for us. The only uncertainty was when they would see us coming and open fire. We walked more briskly than the day before since we had learned that the closer we got to them before they opened fire, the better off we'd be.

When we approached to about 100 yards from the edge of the woods, I signaled to form a skirmish line so we wouldn't have to do so while under fire. I had my M-1 at the ready and resolved not to repeat my dismal performance of the previous day. At 100 yards, we were about the distance from the enemy at which they began to fire at us the morning before. As I walked, I bent forward a bit so I'd be nearer the ground when they opened fire. Although I was apprehensive, I wasn't filled with an overwhelming fear. I might have been thinking, "What if burp gun fire gets me in the chest and then my face as I'm falling?" or "Might a shot to the head through my brain kill me before I hit the ground?" Somehow I had blocked out of my mind such dark thoughts and tried to concentrate on the task at hand, namely to fire back as soon as we were fired upon.

We kept walking ahead silently. Fifty yards from the edge. Twenty-five yards. Suddenly the silence was broken. "They're not here," half shouted one of our men who was a little ahead of the rest of us. The Germans had pulled back and I still wonder why. It was like getting a last minute reprieve from a death sentence.

Just inside the woods were the abandoned foxholes that the Germans had dug to defend against our attack. But we knew that if we didn't meet them here, they would challenge us later on. We, therefore, remained in our skirmish line so that we formed a front at least 100 yards wide sweeping slowly ahead. This formation assured us that we would not inadvertently bypass a German strong point and be fired upon from the rear.

Two Sherman tanks were assigned to the company in the event we needed support in the attack. They were back in

Strass. As the scenario played out, we didn't need them, but strangely we were not enthusiastic about having tanks near us because they attracted enemy fire. Tankers, however, wanted infantry near them, especially in a wooded area because they were afraid of enemy infantry attacking them with *Panzer-fausts*[11] or bazookas.[12]

How could a plain unarmored infantryman protect a heavily armored tank from an anti-tank rocket? Here's how. The tank when "buttoned up" had very limited vision. Therefore, an enemy with a rocket could hide in a hole or a fold in the ground and not be seen by the tankers. But an infantryman could search out and find the enemy infantryman with the rocket and get him by grenade or small arms fire before he had he opportunity to use his anti-tank weapon.

We spent the entire day moving cautiously through the woods in our skirmish line and meeting nary a German. As night started to fall, we came upon a house that had been destroyed from shell fire leaving only the basement intact covered by the flooring above. We decided to spend the night there. Of course one shell could have killed us all, but we had little choice. We could have dug foxholes to sleep in, but we would have had to search for logs in the dark to cover them for protection against tree bursts. I remember the house vividly, because we had to climb down a ladder to get into the basement, which consisted of one large room without any windows.

---

[11]The Panzerfaust was a German anti-tank projectile that looked like a rocket. It was fired once, then discarded.

[12]The bazooka, as most people know, was a hollow metal tube about four feet long. It was loaded by inserting a rocket from the rear. The bazooka rested on the shoulder of the man firing it. When the firer got the target in the sights, he would then press the trigger, and the rocket would be ejected toward the target. The rocket would not be propelled by an explosion like an artillery or rifle round but by the thrust generated within the rocket when it was fired and, I think, as it flew through the air. The advantage of a bazooka over an anti-tank gun is that one man could carry and fire a projectile as powerful as a large anti-tank gun, which required several men to operate and maneuver. The bazooka team had a second man who carried and loaded the rockets.

There were about fifty or sixty of us (the forty men in the brick house plus those who did not make it to the brick house, including the fifteen in the mortar section), so the room was crowded. The only light was from candles and a few flashlights. We posted guards outside, but the rest of us spent the night in the basement.

About halfway through the night, I got stomach cramps and had to go to the bathroom, which was the great outdoors. I found a flashlight and made my way across the prostrate bodies of the sleeping men, up the ladder to ground level. I had the GIs, which is short for the GI shits, an army euphemism for diarrhea, which I had for the next few days. The frequent visits outside necessitated the use of more and more toilet paper, reducing my supply and testing to the limit my toilet paper supply system of keeping the precious stuff at all times in both my shirt pocket and helmet liner. I slept very little and must have climbed up and down that ladder four or five times that night, receiving my share of expletives from the sleeping men I walked over in the basement.

Every time I stepped on someone, he would say, "What the hell ya doin'?" or "Get off my leg, ya dumb shit" or "Get away, ya jerk" or possibly, "What's goin' on?"

These remarks are not startling when you consider the circumstances of men being awakened by someone stepping on them. The unusual part is that the remarks were being directed by the men in the company toward one of their officers, who, if the men realized who was stepping on them, would have been addressed as "Lieutenant" or "Sir" and without the accompanying expletives. On the other hand, I might be overestimating the importance some of the men might have attached to their officers. At least some of them would probably have used the same expletives even if they'd known that the person stepping on them was Dwight D. Eisenhower.

The next couple days, instead of advancing, we were ordered to stay where we were. I was so sick and weak from the GIs that I had one of the men help me back to Strass to the battalion aid station. They gave me a spoonful of medicine and sent me to the basement to sleep on a cot. I slept like a log all day and felt stronger when I woke up late in the afternoon. I went back to the company and found that I had not missed a thing.

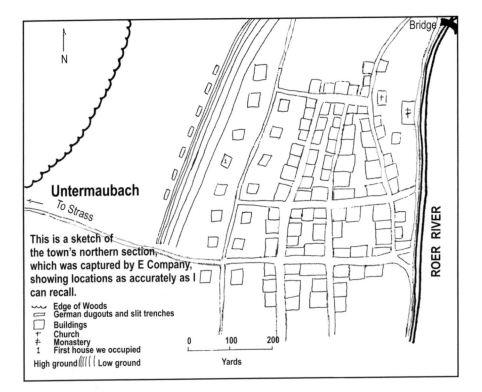

N

Bridge

Untermaubach

To Strass

This is a sketch of
the town's northern section,
which was captured by E Company,
showing locations as accurately as I
can recall.

⌇ Edge of Woods
⌐ German dugouts and slit trenches
▢ Buildings
† Church
⸸ Monastery
1 First house we occupied

High ground ⎰⎰⎰⎰ Low ground

ROER RIVER

0   100   200

Yards

Chapter Seven

Untermaubach
December 1944

Attack into Untermaubach

A FEW MORNINGS LATER WE LEFT the relative safety of the basement and moved through the woods to its eastern edge, which overlooked Untermaubach, a small town on the Roer River. The Roer was the final objective of the entire 83rd Division's attack through the Hürtgen. Untermaubach was surrounded by high ground on all sides except for the side adjoining the river. Across the river, the land was the same elevation as the town. We had a saucer-like view with the town being the middle of the saucer.

Our orders were to attack and capture the town. We suffered no casualties in our attack past the brick house and into the woods, so we still had only one rifle platoon, and I was the leader.

A dense fog covered the town and the approaches to it. At about 8:00 A.M. the company commenced the attack, leaving the edge of the woods in two parallel single columns. Both columns consisted of one squad. The third squad was in the rear as reserve. I waited in the woods, intending to proceed after the first few men had advanced.

One might ask why I wouldn't be at the very front of the platoon. We have seen movies showing George Custer leading the Seventh Cavalry as they advanced toward the Little Big Horn. I suspect that the answer is that we saw Custer in the movies, not in real life. Each rifle squad had two scouts whose job it was to precede the squad in an approach march situation, that is, the period before the enemy is sighted. If the leader were in the very front, he might be picked off by an enemy sniper or be pinned down so that he couldn't get back to direct the attack.

After the scouts had advanced about a hundred yards out of the woods, the fog lifted suddenly. The scene before me was a flat, open field for about 150 yards, and then the land dipped downward into the town. The Germans had dug in at and started firing from the 150 yard mark. Because the terrain changed from a flat surface to a rather steep down grade into the town, this was the last place from which they could defend against an attack from the woods. Our men returned the fire. By that time I was in the middle of the field. I crawled over to one of the squad leaders, a sergeant, and told him that he and I would run up to the front to direct the attack. "Sergeant," I said, "we've got to get up there right away. You go ahead, and I'll follow. We've got to knock out that fire. Move fast and keep your head down. Good luck."

The sergeant ran forward. When he had got about halfway there, he spun around and fell to the ground. "Oh, they got him," I thought. "Well here goes," I said to myself, and I started to get up.

Just then he shook his head, got up, and continued to run forward to where the most advanced men were pinned down. I waited until the sergeant got there, and then I ran across the field to him. "What happened?" I asked.

I'm okay," he replied. "But look at my helmet."

It had two holes in it, one where a bullet had entered and the other where the bullet had exited. This was another miracle like Bonnet's helmet incident in Normandy.

"Boy, that was a close one," I said. "Are you hurt?"

"No, I'm all right. But that was too Goddamn close! You go first next time!"

I was a little startled by this remark, but this was no time for quibbling over who would go first. Another inch to the right and that bullet would have gone through the sergeant's brain. I should have been glad that he stayed and continued to do his job. I was lucky that he didn't look at his helmet and say, "That's enough. I quit. I'm leaving. I'll see ya after this war's over."

Half of the company was with me, and the rest were still in the woods with Packer, since the German fire was too heavy for them to get across the open field to join us. I was against the outside of a German dugout keeping my head down away from the enemy fire. We had taken four or five Germans out of that dugout, but there were other dugouts and slit trenches nearby from which the Germans were firing. Although I would be stretching it a bit to say I was having a good time, I don't think I was terribly frightened, probably because I was so busy trying to dislodge the Germans. To the contrary, for some reason, I was surprisingly calm during the entire attack. I gave orders without hesitation as if I had been doing this all my life. I felt relaxed and comfortable in directing a firefight from the middle of it all with small arms fire whizzing by us from both sides and German mortar and artillery fire keeping us hitting the ground.

We took the first dugout by fire and movement. We directed sufficient fire against it to allow one of our men to get close enough to throw a grenade into or near the dugout's entrance. This brought the Germans out with their hands raised. The prisoners were sent to the rear later in the day, since no one was crossing the open field back into the woods because of the small arms fire coming from both sides of the field.

I called back to Packer on the radio, "We're stuck here and can't get 'em out. There's so much fire, we can't get to 'em. Can ya get a couple tanks up here to help? The quicker, the better."

"Yeah", said Packer. "We've got some right behind us. They'll be on their way in no time."

Within half an hour, two Sherman tanks came out of the woods to our position. The lead tank stopped near me. The hatch on top of the tank opened and the tank commander stood up. I was standing in front of the tank under the barrel of its 75-millimeter gun. I said to the commander, "See those dugouts over there? That's where the fire's coming from."

He closed the hatch quickly and before I could move off to the side, they fired the "75." I was right under the barrel and the muzzle blast from the gun knocked me to the ground. I got to my feet and moved away, and except for the buzzing in my ears from the concussion, I was all right. That was fifty years ago, and I remember the incident well. It was no fun.

Soon after this, a German shell exploded near me. Upon hearing the whistle of the shell coming in, I hit the ground and was flat on my face at the time of the explosion. I felt a stinging sensation in my back. I thought that I had been hit, so I took off my field jacket and pulled up my sweater and shirt and underwear and asked Martinson if he could see where I had been hit. "Marty, I think that one got me in the back," I said while pulling up my shirt. "Do ya see anything"

"No, Lieutenant," he said, "nothing but a real skinny back."

I immediately felt better.

With the help of the tanks, we cleared most of the bunkers and slit trenches on the edge of Untermaubach. After this the tanks went back. We took a few prisoners, but the rest of the Germans retreated into the town, so we continued the attack down into it. From the bunkers and slit trenches, we advanced down the slope toward a row of houses that were about 100 yards from the high ground. A few of our men got into the first house they neared. (See map on page 130.) At the same time, there was intermittent small arm's fire coming from the Germans.

The German small arms consisted of rifles, machine guns, and burp guns (MP40s), which were small all-metal machine pistols (with a metal rather than wooden stock) and which were somewhat comparable to our grease gun and our Thompson sub-machine gun (Tommy gun). The German automatic weapons, the machine gun, and the burp gun, were distinguishable from our automatic weapons, the machine gun, the BAR, the grease gun, and the Tommy gun, by the more rapid rate of fire of the German guns. Whereas the American automatic weapon's fire sounded like "chug-chug-chug," the German machine gun responded with, "da-da-da-da," and the burp gun went even faster, "burrr-urp, burrr-urp, burrr-urp," with each burp being several rounds. We could always tell from the sound whether the fire was German or American.

To reach the first house, I had to run across about fifty yards of an open field. A deep ditch ran through the field, and in order to cross it, there were three or four long planks laid loosely across the ditch forming a bridge. As I ran across, my right leg slipped between two of the boards, and I fell heavily to the bridge. I was stuck with my leg dangling through the boards. The force from the fall centered on my right thigh, which became completely numb, and I was sure the thigh bone was broken. I tried to get up but couldn't. I felt like I was the only target in a shooting gallery. I thought the Germans could see me, but for some reason they didn't fire—or, if they did, they missed. After what seemed like hours, but was actually only a minute or two, the feeling returned to my leg. I pulled it out from between the boards, got up, and ran to the house.

When I got to the house, one of my men said, "Lieutenant, what happened? I thought you were hit."

"I slipped on a board on that little bridge. I thought I broke my leg. Those Germans are supposed to be good shots. What happened?"

"I don't know. I don't think they saw you right away, but just before you got up, I saw a few puffs of dirt fly up behind you. You're lucky. They missed."

Only fifteen to twenty men got to the house with me, while the rest of the company was on the higher ground surrounding the town. They couldn't get through the German fire to reach us, so our little band was cut off from the rest of the company. When it started to get dark, Packer called me over the radio, "Devitt, this is Packer. Colonel Norris says you can bring your men out of there before it gets too dark. But you can stay if you want." Since we'd spent all day getting into the town, I didn't want to withdraw and then replay the scene the next day. So, I told Packer in effect, "Thanks, but no thanks." I said, "I don't want to fight all over again tomorrow just to get back here. We'll stay. See ya in the morning. Bring plenty of chow. Roger. Out."

The night was fairly quiet. We were afraid that the Germans, if they realized how few of us there were in the house, might try a counterattack, but they didn't. All that I recall about that night is that I slept in the basement in either a potato bin or coal bin.

Attack within Untermaubach - The First Day

On the edge of the town were stucco houses with yards and gardens. All the civilians had fled. Toward the center of town, the buildings were built up to the street and usually attached to each other. Several streets ran to the Roer River, while others ran parallel to it. It was a small town through which it would take no more than five minutes to walk. It took us three days. The going is slower while under fire by a hostile force.

Early the next morning, before full daylight, the rest of the company joined us without drawing any or much German fire.

One advantage the Germans had over us was that they had smokeless powder in their small arms ammunition. When the Americans fired a rifle, B.A.R, grease gun, Tommy gun, or machine gun, smoke would rise from the weapon, so our location could be spotted by the Germans. On the other hand, when they fired at us, we often couldn't determine their position because their weapons did not emit smoke. I remember wondering why we did not have smokeless powder, and, at a later date, I asked someone. The answer I received was that smokeless powder damaged the barrel of the rifle so that it would wear out more quickly. If that were the reasoning, it was poor, probably made by someone who had no experience in infantry fighting. The small arms used by infantry had a very short life expectancy. Almost every time that a man was wounded or killed, his weapon was left on the ground where he fell. These weapons generally were not damaged by overuse, but by disuse—they were left on the ground and deteriorated. I wonder how many American soldiers' lives were lost through the false economy of not using smokeless powder.

Since the whole company occupied only a single house, our plan of attack was simple—attack the houses nearest us. During the first day we attacked and occupied about a dozen houses near the first one. We didn't get much resistance from within the houses, but German small arms' fire, which we had trouble locating because of the smokeless powder and which came from some distance away, slowed our advance.

I still remember, upon entering the first house, seeing a loaf of German rye bread on the kitchen table. There were a few slices lying on the table. It was very dark in color, with a strong vinegar-like odor. We had disrupted the German soldiers' lunch. I speculated at the time why the Germans seemed to eat their normal food while we had all sorts of special rations in boxes and cans. One reason might have been that we were often attacking, so that it was difficult to bring hot food to men who were frequently moving forward.

After the war ended, I had an opportunity to sample some dehydrated potato flakes that the Germans provided to their soldiers. The flakes were mixed with water and heated, and the result was an almost unpalatable version of mashed potatoes. So the German soldiers didn't always have the tastiest food any more than we did.

About all that I remember of the first day's attack was setting up a machine gun under a large window in a house. There was an open field of fire outside the house, and I thought the machine gun would be more effective raised up above ground level, where the gun would normally be placed. I was careful to have the gun several feet back from the window, so it could not be seen from outside. I had learned from my training (possibly as far back as St. Thomas) that by staying back away from a window, the shadows within the room would prevent someone at a distance from seeing objects in the room. I also remember that we did not fire the machine gun from within the room, because the Germans had pulled back. Nevertheless, I still think that I had a pretty good idea in setting up the gun. I was somewhat proud of my plan.

The Second Day

By the end of the first day, we had occupied only about a dozen houses. By the end of the second day, we had taken most of the town. Lest one should think that E Company was winning the war all by itself, I should add that another of the battalion's rifle companies came into the town on the second day, and attacked from the south of us. This was G Company, and the company commander was Captain Jim Wright, a fine fellow, a West Pointer, who was killed while leading his company in its attack on Untermaubach. I don't know the circumstances surrounding his death. Someone simply told me a few hours after it happened that he had been killed.

Most of the fighting on the second day took place near the center of the town, where the buildings were built up to the street and were all attached to each other. We would have one group of men on either side of the street. While some men fired to keep the Germans from firing at us, we would charge the front of the building and throw a grenade or two into a window or a door, wait for the explosions, and then rush inside. If any German soldiers were in the building, they would either surrender, be killed or wounded, or retreat further into the town. After a building was cleared of German soldiers, we would go out the front door and down the street to the next building. In this way, we cleared most of the town on the second day.

Sometimes when we came to a building in which we thought Germans still remained, we would call out a phrase, which sounded like, "Come out *mit der handen haupen.*" We thought that this meant, "Come out with the hands raised." I don't know who came up with this phrase, or what, if anything, it means. But it did seem to work, for sometimes the response would be German soldiers emerging from the embattled building with their hands raised in surrender. As I learned later, all Germans take English in school and many speak and understand it quite well. So we probably would have done better if we had spoken English instead of our manufactured German.

I was with one group that had just cleared a building. I carefully put my head out the front door and peered down the street to the next building. Just as I looked out, a head in the front door of that building cautiously appeared and looked at me. We were no more than fifty feet apart. We stared at each other for a moment, and then we both seemed to realize at the same time that he was a German soldier and I an American and that there was a war going on and that we should do something. He ran out the door and started running up the street away from me. I stepped out and fired away at him. I missed, and, the last I saw of him, he was skittering over the hill at the end of the street, like Charlie Chaplin in an old silent movie.

One of our tanks was brought up to help us. The tank was in the middle of the street, and I was standing a few feet to one side, next to a building. Without warning, the tank was struck in the front by a rocket from a German bazooka. I looked down the street where it changed to a Y intersection and saw two or three German soldiers with the bazooka. From the size of the explosion, I thought that the tank was knocked out. But a moment later the tank backed up a few feet and then fired its 75-mm gun at the German bazooka crew. It was an unequal contest. When we got to the Y intersection, we saw that the Germans were killed and their bazooka blown to pieces.

Those were truly brave German soldiers. They risked, and lost, their lives attempting to destroy an American tank that was sure to get them unless their first shot knocked it out. The irony of the incident is that if such bravery had been demonstrated by Americans, they would have been acclaimed as heroes. In fact, our division had a standing order that any man who knocked out a German tank with a bazooka would be promoted to sergeant. But we were the victors, not the losers. I suspect that those dead Germans were never recognized for their bravery. With a little luck, the German rocket might have hit the tank at a slightly different angle or in its turret, thereby disabling the tank and allowing the brave Germans to survive.

We took many prisoners the second day in Untermaubach. We held them in a room in one of the buildings until we accumulated enough of them to warrant the use of two or three of our men to escort them to the rear. I remember looking into the room and seeing that it was filled with German soldiers, probably thirty or forty. They were as dirty and miserable and tired of fighting as we were. In a way, they were luckier than we. For them, the war was over. But for us, the victorious American infantry, the future remained bleaker. Our most realistic hope for getting out of the war was to be wounded (we hoped not very badly) and evacuated. Of course, there was the good chance of being fatally wounded, but not even the most morbid among us wanted that. I don't think that I ever consciously wished to be wounded, although I frequently wished to be out of combat. By this stage in my combat experience I

I believe this is the radioman (below) for the E Company headquarters in Untermaubach. He was using the SCR 300 radio. December 1944. (Photo courtesy of the 83rd Infantry Division Association)

The above photograph reminds me of the tank incident in Untermaubach. The American tank's 75 mm gun is pointing towards the German bazooka crew, and our men are looking for the enemy. This picture might have been taken in Untermaubach, but, while I was there, the action was so hot and heavy that a photographer would have concentrated on keeping his head down rather than snapping pictures. December 1944. (Photo courtesy of 83rd Infantry Division Association)

had a feeling that I was just lucky, somehow led a charmed life, and was immune from the wounds of battle suffered by most front-line infantrymen.

I hadn't any feelings against the German prisoners, even though only moments before being captured they had been trying to kill me. But I was, and still am, upset at such a civilized people as the Germans for tolerating their terrible political system, and their evil führer, Adolf Hitler. Perhaps my attitude toward the German soldier would have been more hate-filled if my combat experience had been different. Most of the casualties I observed came from indirect fire, from mortars and artillery, which was fired, not by the German soldiers we were fighting, but rather by some faceless individuals in the rear. I never participated in a battle like Gettysburg, in the Civil War, in which large masses of infantry fought hand to hand using whatever weapons were available, including the bayonet and the clenched fist. Instead I felt much empathy for the poor German foot soldier, who was in the same boat as I was.

The Third Day - Schacher

Paul Schacher was the oldest man in the third platoon. He was thirty-two years old, whereas I was twenty-one, which was close to the average age of the men. He was from North Carolina. I think he was married, and through some sort of fluke got into a rifle company. The physical and emotional stress of combat with the infantry made youth a desirable quality for survival. We considered Schacher an old man and wondered how he kept up. He was one of the few members of the third platoon who was still with us from the time we had entered the Hürtgen.

On the third day, one of the first problems we faced was how to get across a road to a building on the other side. We had faced this situation many times before. Usually, someone would just run across the road and then signal for the others to follow. But this time for some reason no one went first. I could have just ordered one of the men to cross and hope that he made it.

Instead of ordering one of the men to cross the road, I asked if anyone would volunteer to go first. The men were understandably reluctant to volunteer. "Who'll volunteer," I said. "Who'll go across first? We'll all follow after someone checks it out. Volunteer anyone?"

Schacher put up his hand, "I'll go, Lieutenant."

"Good," I said. "I don't see anyone over there, but move fast and keep your head down. Look around and signal when it's clear. Okay. Get going."

Here was this old man showing up all the younger fellows. Schacher ran across safely, and, after making sure that there were no German soldiers nearby, he signaled for us to follow, and we did.

It might be asked why I didn't cross the road first. Perhaps I should have. I don't think that it was fear that caused me not to go first. I thought that it was best to send one of the men and take the chance of losing him, rather than endangering myself. I realize that this sounds like the explanation of someone who was afraid to risk his own neck and had the power to risk someone else's. I learned fairly early in the game, however, that a dead leader cannot lead.

Although I think I took my fair share of the perils in combat, I usually had in mind (often subconsciously) the balance between the importance of the risks I was considering and my possible loss to the company. I can hear someone chuckling at this explanation and saying, "Who the hell did you think you were? Napoleon?"

By the beginning of the third day of our attack in Untermaubach, we had taken most of the town. The Germans still held the buildings close to the Roer River as well as the bridge crossing it.

We decided to try to take the bridge first. It was located about 100 yards north of the center of the town and had only a few buildings near it. In order to get there, it was necessary to cross an open field fifty to a 100 yards wide. While some men fired, others sprinted across in a single dash to get to cover on the other side. The German fire was light, so the first few men reached the other side safely.

Then I decided to go. I was still so sick and weak from the GIs that I could not run, but instead walked as fast as I could. Unknown to me, Colonel Norris, the battalion commander, was observing our operation from back on the high ground. I learned later that he remarked favorably about the brave lieutenant who calmly walked across the open field in the face of enemy fire. Of course he didn't know that such "bravery" was aided, abetted, and directly caused by a severe case of the GIs.

As we got close to the bridge, it blew up with a roar. The Germans had mined it and then detonated it to prevent our taking it and crossing to the other side.

I wonder now what we would have done if the Germans had not blown the bridge. One's first inclination might have been to cross it to prevent the Germans from destroying it, but I'm sure that Packer or I would have called Colonel Norris to ask him what to do. I think that he would have told us to stay on our side of the river. Trying to cross to the other side and hold on with the few men left in the company until reinforcements arrived would have been an invitation to disaster.

We turned to our last objective, the buildings near the river. The Germans were firing from a church that overlooked the river, and we returned the fire. After we achieved fire superiority, we rushed forward and got inside. By this time the Germans had had enough, and a large number, perhaps forty to fifty, surrendered. I went to one of the windows overlooking the river, and down below on the street abutting the river were a number of German soldiers who had no place to go. The bridge was blown, and they had run out of space in the town. We called down to them to surrender, and they did, since, as they said in the old cowboy movies, "We had the drop on 'em."

This ended E Company's attack on Untermaubach. I estimate that we took a hundred prisoners on the third day.

Late in the day we were relieved by another unit, and the company left town. We walked out single file. Packer led the company, and I was the last man in the rear. If we had not been relieved by another company, we soon would have ceased being an effective fighting force, since with the daily loss of men caused by the determined German resistance, we would have just run out of men to do the fighting.

Of the approximately 180 enlisted men who entered the Hürtgen, there were probably fewer than forty who walked out of Untermaubach that day. Of the seven officers who had been with the company before the battle began, Packer and I were the only ones left. One had been injured before we entered, one was killed, and three were wounded.

I can't account for all of the losses we suffered. Some men were evacuated because of illness, frostbite, or trenchfoot, and a few might just have got "lost" from the company, intentionally or otherwise, but by far the greatest number of men were either killed or wounded.

I do know that for three straight weeks, I saw men killed or wounded almost every day. It would be difficult to exaggerate the physical and emotional pain that surrounded us. All the time, day and night, we had the continuing fear that a mortar or artillery shell could explode on or near us. In fact, after E Company had passed through Strass and the town was not within direct observation of the enemy, a shell landed on the back of a trailer in a small courtyard, killing several American soldiers.

The German small arms' fire took a heavy toll when we attacked. After dark, when we'd be exhausted from attacking all day, we'd have to find or dig a hole, or, if lucky, crawl into a basement, and try to get some rest to be prepared for the next day's go around. When things quieted down, we'd tear open a package of cold K-rations and try to enjoy an icy breakfast, lunch or dinner. Even after we found a place to sleep, we were always uncomfortable from the cold, or freezing rain or drizzle, or snow. Life was pure misery.

When we attacked, the enemy small arms' fire was often deadly. I cannot reiterate enough, the bravery shown by each front-line infantryman just by doing his job. Whenever we attacked, every man would risk his life when he got off the ground and moved forward. Further, every man who stood his ground during a mortar or artillery barrage risked his life by doing so. They often gave medals for risking one's life in combat. But if that were the standard used to give medals to front-line infantrymen, each would have earned a half dozen medals a day.

If I were asked what is the most important characteristic of a good front-line infantryman, I think that my answer would be that he followed orders. He did what he was told to do. That sounds overly simple and unrealistic. Of course all soldiers follow orders. But the difference between the front-line infantryman and most other soldiers was that in following his orders, the front-line infantryman was often risking death, laying his life on the line, which was not the case for most of the others. Obeying orders for the front-line infantryman was not merely having his shoes shined for an inspection or changing a tire on a motor pool Jeep, but was risking getting his head shot off in an attack or receiving a piece of hot shrapnel in the belly.

The living conditions alone, without the threat of enemy fire, were bad enough to make one ill. We slept in a hole in the ground, or in the basement of an unheated, damaged, abandoned building. We had no hot food, no change of clothing, no baths, and no place to be warm. The weather was in the thirties and forties Fahrenheit during the day, and colder at night. There was intermittent rain and an occasional snow flurry. Some days were sunny, and some were not. In Minnesota, we would have thought of this as mild winter weather. But in Minnesota we live in houses, and in winter those houses are heated.

A few hours before writing this paragraph, I saw on television Kristi Yamaguchi, a lovely American girl, win the gold medal in women's figure skating in the 1992 Winter Olympics in Albertville, France. In the ceremony at which she received the medal for herself and her country, she stood on a podium with the American flag behind her and with the national anthem playing on the loudspeaker. The television camera showed many in the audience in tears at this emotional scene as it recorded the thunderous cheers for Kristi and her remarkable accomplishment.

I watched near tears myself at the sight of a young American woman being honored for acquitting herself so magnificently for her country.

What a contrast to the complete lack of recognition to the small group of men from E Company who walked out of Untermaubach, and to the much larger contingent from E Company who had been killed or wounded in the Hürtgen! Of course, there could have been no such recognition at the time. How does one thank men who, for weeks, risked their lives daily—often hourly—for their country? There is no way to express completely and adequately the country's gratitude to

Futch, Sandler, Elliott, Wright, and the others who died, to Bonnet, Chambers, Kurek, Vitulo, Berry, Brill, White, Colonel Foster, Haney, Wooldridge, and the others who were wounded, and to Packer, Schacher, and the few remaining members of the company who walked out of Untermaubach.

Ironic as it appears, it's not surprising that the rewards arising from winning an Olympic gold medal and from suffering through the Hürtgen Forest battle seems inversely proportional to the risk to life involved.

Christmas in the Cave

After leaving Untermaubach, we walked only a few hundred yards to a cave that had been dug into the side of a hill. The entire company stayed in the cave that night and part of the next day, which was Christmas.

The cave had plenty of head room to walk around and enough space for the forty or so men to sleep. Of course it was pitch black, so we lighted candles, and a few men started small fires to take the chill out of the air. Needless to say, we were soon in a *very* smoke-filled room, but, curiously, I don't think that anyone minded. If it got too bad for someone, he could go outside and get some fresh air. But we had had plenty of fresh air over the last few weeks, so we tended to stay in the cave.

I remember thinking how appropriate it was that we should spend Christmas in a cave. More important, however, we weren't being shot at. On Christmas day, the mess sergeant and his crew brought us the traditional hot Christmas dinner with turkey and the trimmings. A hamburger would have been a treat, but a hot turkey dinner was almost beyond belief.

While in the cave, one of the men told me that he heard that I had been recommended for the Distinguished Service Cross (or DSC, the second highest medal for bravery that the army awards, behind the Congressional Medal of Honor). He said that Colonel Norris had put me in for it for my action in crossing the field while attacking toward the bridge in Untermaubach, an action the colonel had observed. I was both puzzled and skeptical. I didn't think that I deserved the DSC, so I couldn't understand why I would have been cited for such a high commendation. I also thought that the informant might have got his information from an unreliable source. I could have asked Packer what he knew about it, but I didn't, probably because I did not want to take it very seriously. Nevertheless, I felt good about the prospect of getting such a high medal and looked forward to hearing further.

Several weeks later, I heard that I had received the Bronze Star, the lowest medal for bravery. I confess that I was very disappointed. I had thought that if I had been recommended for a citation, I probably wouldn't get a DSC, but hoped that it would be a Silver Star, which ranked between the DSC and the Bronze Star.

But, as the French say with a shrug, "*C'est la guerre.*"

Out of the Hürtgen

Right after Christmas, we got into trucks and rode to the city of Aachen, about thirty miles away. As we drove through the Hürtgen Forest to Aachen, we noticed the absence of our tanks on the road. When we had entered the Hürtgen a few weeks earlier, the roads had been lined with American tanks waiting for us to punch through the forest so that they could get to the open ground beyond the Roer River. But now the tanks were gone. What happened?

On December 16th, the Germans attacked the American lines to the south of us and had broken through in what was later called "The Battle of the Bulge." Our tanks had pulled out to defend against that attack.

Epilogue to this Chapter

After the war in Europe ended, the 83rd Division had a contest in which each of the division's nine battalions submitted narratives on three different types of combat in which they all had participated. These were village fighting, attack on a fortified position, and one other, which I cannot recall. Lieutenant Colonel Norris, my battalion commander, assigned me the village fighting topic using the Untermaubach battle. He gave himself one of the other two, and another officer in the battalion got the third.

I won the village fighting topic, and Colonel Norris won his. So our battalion won two of the three. The prize for each topic was the choice of a vacation in England, the French Riveria, or Switzerland. When Colonel Norris advised me that I had won, I told him that I chose Switzerland. He said to me, "You really don't want to go, do you?"

I answered, "Yes, sir, I really do."

He replied, "Well, I can't let you go right now. We're in the middle of training, and we have to lick Japan before this war's over."

Since Colonel Norris also won a prize, he probably didn't consider it much of an achievement to have won. He didn't take his prize either. A few weeks later, Japan surrendered, the war was over, and I went home. As a result, the closest I've gotten to Switzerland is a recent issue of *National Geographic.*

I don't even have a copy of the narrative. When I began this chapter on Untermaubach, I looked for my copy, but to no avail. I tried to obtain a copy from the 83rd Division records in St. Louis, but I learned that the records had been destroyed in a fire several years before.

I wonder if I should contact the Pentagon and tell them my sad story and say that I *really, really* wanted to see Switzerland. Perhaps I could bring tears to the eyes of some caring colonel who might manage to reinstate my prize.

Chapter Eight

Belgium - The Battle of the Bulge
January 1945

The Hot Shower

WHILE IN AACHEN, FOR THE FIRST TIME in a month we had clean clothes as well as showers. We had to stand in line for the showers, and Packer and I were at the end of the line. There were three or four showerheads for the company's use. Each man savored his shower and spent much more than the normal time under the steamy, warm water. We had taken our dirty clothes off, and were standing naked, eagerly anticipating the cleansing with soapy, warm water. The area in which we waited was rather cool and drafty, but the anticipation of bathing distracted me from feeling the cold. Finally, my turn came. I stepped under the showerhead and turned on the water. At first it was slightly warm, but then it turned ice cold! They had run out of hot water! Mine was probably the quickest shower in the company.

The Big Sleep

After a day or so in Aachen, we again set off in trucks, this time headed for Belgium. It was dark when we left, and the weather was cold with blowing snow. The convoy consisted of the entire Second Battalion with E Company in about the middle and with twenty to thirty trucks in all. We were driving under blackout conditions. That meant that the normal headlights and taillights were not on, but instead the lights were narrow slits (called cat's eyes) which threw little light and were hard to see. The trucks had to drive close behind each other in order to see the one in front.

Each truck had a cab for a driver and a passenger. The cab was enclosed with a top and windows and, most importantly, had a heater. The trucks held about twenty men. There were benchlike seats along each side where some of the men sat, and the balance sat on the floor in the middle. The back of the truck had a canvas top that ordinarily protected against the elements and, with enough men, could make the temperature inside a little warmer than the outside. Unfortunately, however, we were not allowed to use the canvas top for fear that if a truck turned over on one of the icy roads, the men, instead of being thrown clear, would be crushed within the canvas top.

As an officer, I had the privilege of sitting in the heated cab with the driver. Along with this privilege came the responsibility of making sure that the driver stayed alert and drove carefully.

After we had been on the road for about two hours, the truck ahead of us stopped, and we stopped immediately behind it. The cab was warm and comfortable. I was tired, and fell asleep for a moment.

When I awoke, I saw the truck ahead of us was gone. I said to the driver, "Where's the truck ahead?"

"I don't know, Lieutenant. I must have dozed off."

"Well, get going." I said. "You'd better drive a little faster so we can catch up. I hope we get to that town soon 'cause the fellows in the back are getting pretty cold."

About half of the convoy was following behind us. All this time the men in the backs of the trucks were getting colder and colder—and more and more unhappy. They were like Eskimo Pies stuffed in a box inside a freezer.

We continued down the road, but did not catch up to the rest of the convoy. After about a half hour, we came to a small town. At the edge of the town we were stopped by an

American soldier, a sentry. He challenged us, asking me for the password. After I gave him the countersign, I told him that we were looking for a certain town, our destination. He told me that the town was half an hour to our rear.

While the driver and I had been asleep, we were stopped outside of our destination. The trucks ahead of us turned into town while we slept, and when we awoke, we continued along the road. After talking to the sentry, we got the convoy turned around and got back to our destination without further delay. I do know that in a popularity poll of the men in the rear of the trucks, I would have come in last place behind Adolf Hitler.

When the Germans broke through the American lines at the beginning of the Battle of the Bulge, there were many stories of German soldiers dressed in American uniforms who had slipped behind American lines. This caused apprehension and fear among people behind the front lines. An example of this occurred when the American sentry challenged me at the edge of the small town while I was busy losing half of the battalion. The roof of my truck's cab had a machine gun mounted on it. As my truck stopped, I stood up in the cab to talk to the sentry and rested my arm on the machine gun. The sentry, fearing that I might be a German in American clothing, said, "Lieutenant, take your hand off that machine gun, or I'll have to shoot you." I sat down promptly.

Our destination was a small rural town and I, together with about five of my men, stayed in a house. We asked the Belgian family if we could spend the night there. They said we could stay in the front room, which was a kitchen with a dining table, a few straight-back chairs, and a wooden bench. I slept on the stone floor, and still recall its unforgiving hardness and cold. Although stone is one of the least desirable surfaces for sleeping comfort, I was nevertheless grateful for being allowed to sleep in a warm, dry house.

Not everyone in the battalion was so fortunate. The next day I was surprised to learn that Colonel Norris, the battalion commander, had slept in a barn that night. I think that if I had been the battalion commander, I would have seen to it that henceforth the battalion commander would have had suitable sleeping quarters. I suspect that Colonel Norris, kindly man that he was, did not make a fuss over his less than comfortable accommodations.

We stayed in the Belgian town for the next few days. We received replacements for the many men we had lost in the Hürtgen. We got two or three officers and enough men to expand the company from one rifle platoon to three, probably between seventy-five and 125 new men.

Not all soldiers' deaths came in battle. The night that the company was being trucked from Aachen to the Belgian town, one of the trucks in the convey carried all of our mess and other equipment including stoves, tents, food, and supplies. The back of the truck was piled high with the cargo so that some of it was three or four feet higher than the cab of the truck. Two of the cooks rode in the back to prevent hungry soldiers from looting the food whenever the convey came to a halt. One of the cooks stationed himself in the rear near the floor of the truck under the canvas that covered the cargo. But the other man for some reason decided to ride near the top of the pile, sinking down into the canvas cover for some protection against the snow and cold.

As the convey approached a low stone bridge that crossed over the road, the convoy commander, who was in the lead vehicle, stopped the convoy and brought up a truck to see if it could make it under the bridge. The truck cleared the bridge with a foot or two to spare, so the commander ordered the convey to proceed under the bridge. Unfortunately, the commander did not realize that our mess truck stuck up higher than any other vehicle in the convoy. Our truck approached the bridge at about thirty miles an hour. The cab cleared the bridge easily, but the top foot of the cargo was too high and smashed into the bridge. The man on the top of the cargo was thrown through the air against the stone bridge abutment and died instantly. What irony! For the last month, he had constantly been within range of the German artillery fire. And now while out of range of the enemy fire and proceeding still farther from it, he was killed. His death shook us up more than the battle deaths because it was so unexpected. But death is death, no matter from whence it comes.

The Buzz Bomb

The V-1 was a German weapon that consisted of an explosive attached to an engine, a sort of pilotless plane, which could be directed at a far away target such as London. It was called a Buzz Bomb from the buzzing noise it made in flight. It sounded like a swarm of bees descending on a nectar-filled flower garden. When it reached its destination, the engine shut off and the V-1 would glide to the ground and explode. It had been used for some time against London, getting more than its share of publicity from the news media. It was not very accurate, but there was always the possibility that bad luck might bring one near people in London or some other heavily populated area. Although we, as soldiers, had heard of the V-1s, we had no fear of them since we thought they were not being directed against us. One day we heard the sound of an engine and looked up and saw a speck in the sky coming in our direction. It was not moving fast, and I didn't even think about taking cover and preparing to fire at it. For a few moments we stood watching it approach, and then the engine cut out, and it glided to an open field out of our sight. The large explosion that followed told us that we had seen our first V-1 and, we hoped, the last. The Germans certainly didn't intend to send a V-1 against such a lightly populated target area, so that V-1 was misdirected or suffered a mechanical failure.

We spent our time trying to make the new men part of a cohesive unit. We had to assign each man to a platoon and a squad, and then try to be sure that all were ready for combat. One of the things we did was to give instructions in each weapon. One day we had all the men assembled for instruction on the use and care of the Browning Automatic Rifle (BAR). One of the veterans, an experienced BAR man, was instructing the recruits in the use of the gun. The BAR had a bolt that slid backward when a shot was fired. The empty "brass" would be ejected and a new round automatically inserted into the breech so that the gun was ready to fire again when the bolt moved forward. As the instructor was showing the men how the bolt worked, it stuck about halfway back.

"Damnit," he said. "The damn bolt's stuck. Whenever you have a problem like this, always point the barrel away from everyone. You can never tell when a round might be in the chamber."

After trying several times to push it with his hand, he put the butt of the rifle on the floor and pushed the bolt handle with his foot. He succeeded in getting it back, but then his foot slipped off the handle and the bolt slammed forward. This caused the round in the chamber to discharge with a bang, and a bullet flew by the instructor's head. It missed him, but not by much. He had pointed the barrel away from everyone but himself.

The Meeting

While in the Belgian town, Colonel Norris called a meeting of all the officers in the battalion. I sat in the group of twenty-five to thirty men feeling very relaxed, for I had nothing to do. When he finished his talk, the colonel suddenly turned to me and said, "Devitt, do you have any ideas or suggestions which might be useful when we get up there again next week? Don't be afraid to speak up. You can never tell when some little thing you learned along the way might be helpful to us all."

I was caught unaware. I wondered why, of all those present, he called only on me. I think there were two reasons. First, I was one of the few, possibly only, rifle platoon leaders in the battalion who made it through the entire Hürtgen Forest campaign. Therefore, I was one of the most experienced men at the meeting. Second, I think he liked me and thought I had done a good job in combat, and might have something useful to say. After some hesitation and hoping for enlightenment, I said, "Well, Colonel, I don't know. About the only thing I can think of is to keep in mind the importance of the BAR. If you lose the BAR man, you can't lose the BAR. So I'd say tell your men that if the BAR man gets hit, be sure that someone else picks it up. And he has to be sure to take the ammo magazines off the old BAR man, or else he'll have the gun, but no ammo."

I left the meeting feeling confident and quietly happy. I was now one of the old-timers.

The Ardennes

On January 2, 1945, we got into trucks again, and E Company went into the Ardennes Forest in Belgium, the area near where the Germans had made their farthest advance in the Battle of the Bulge. Our mission was to counterattack against the northern edge of the German forces that had penetrated through the American lines.

When we were in Luxembourg in September, October, and November, it was a lightly defended area. At that time, to both the north and south of us, the American army was attacking but not making much progress against stubborn German resistance. Earlier in the fall, we heard that we were going to be part of a large attack, the Big Push, but then the weather turned rainy and the attack was called off. I'm sure that our generals hoped for an opportunity to punch through the German defenses, which would allow our tanks to thrust through behind the German lines, similar to what had happened in Normandy in July.

The American attacks in the Hürtgen Forest were for the purpose of getting across the Roer River to the Cologne Plain, which was thought of as tank country. Once on the Cologne Plain, we could take advantage of our numerical superiority in tanks and break through the German lines.

By the time we got to the Roer, the Germans had beaten us to the punch. On December 16, the Germans began their counteroffensive, attacking the American lines just a few miles north of where we had been in Luxembourg a month before.

The German attack was initially against several American divisions. One of the divisions was the 106th, which had recently come from the United States and, being inexperienced, was placed in that quiet holding position on the line. Another, the Fourth, was the veteran division that we had replaced in the Hürtgen. The Fourth Division was sent to that quiet sector to lick its wounds and get replacements for the losses it had suffered in the Hürtgen.

The Germans had planned their counteroffensive for several weeks. The plan was quite simple. They would break through the American lines at the weakly held positions in Luxembourg and send specially trained troops behind the American lines to disrupt the movement of reinforcements. They would use tanks to drive through to Liege and finally to Antwerp, thereby splitting the bulk of the American forces to the south from the English forces to the north. If they succeeded, the German leaders hoped that the Americans and British might agree to a negotiated peace, separate from the Russians.

The chances of the Germans reaching Antwerp were slight, and their chances of a separate negotiated peace were even less. But what concerned me then, and what still concerns me, is how the Germans were able to break through our lines before we were able to break through theirs.

Years ago I read books by Generals Omar Bradley and Dwight D. Eisenhower about the war in Europe. They both said that the Germans were able to accomplish the breakthrough because the Americans took a calculated risk. The calculated risk was the reduction of our defenses in Luxembourg in order to provide more forces where we were attacking. Bradley and Eisenhower made the Battle of the Bulge sound like a great American victory. They even claimed that it shortened the war. Perhaps it did. But what really happened, I believe, is that the Germans out-generalled us. They waited until the weather became snowy for a number of days, which prevented our air force from flying and detecting German troop movements. Then they concentrated a large force against our lightly held section and smashed through our lines.

I think that our generals (in connection with the German breakthrough) did a lot of risking but not enough calculating. Didn't the Germans also have to take calculated risks? Why the Germans were able to break through our lines before we could break through theirs still puzzles me.

Esprit de Corps

Esprit de Corps (literally, in French, the spirit of the body or group) is defined in *The American Heritage Dictionary of the English Language* as, "A common spirit of devotion and enthusiasm among members of a group."

The 83rd Division was a fairly new one, having been reactivated in 1942 after its formation during World War I. The regular army divisions—the ones with lower numbers, such as the First, Second, Third and Fourth Infantry Divisions—had stayed, I believe, active since World War I. They, therefore, had a long history and tradition to uphold, something which the newer divisions, which constituted the bulk of the army, did not have.

When men joined these regular army divisions, usually they were told of the division's history and tradition in an attempt to give them a feeling of pride in the unit, an *esprit de corps*. This is important for an infantry unit in combat. For men to fight well, they must be motivated. Traditionally, the great motivator was fear, fear of retribution by the officers, and fear of scorn by one's fellow soldiers. But when, in battle, some usual motivations fade, such as patriotism or fear of retribution (which could be canceled out by the fear of death in combat), then, it was hoped, *esprit de corps*, and the desire not to let down the other men in the unit, would bring forth the best in soldiers to do their duty by risking their lives.

I don't know whether the 83rd Division was less effective because of the absence of history and tradition.

Whenever we attacked, we did so because we had received orders directing us. I never had a great urge to get at the enemy; to the contrary, I was always afraid and apprehensive before an attack. Except for Sandler's heroic action and his men's swift reaction to his death and White's performance on the tank, I don't believe that any of us in E Company during my time with them evidenced enthusiasm to get at the enemy. I never felt a surge of patriotism that propelled me forward against the foe. Patriotism is a feeling that can be overwhelming while watching the Olympic games or viewing a parade of veterans of a recently concluded war. But to the infantryman facing the enemy eyeball to eyeball, patriotism was the farthest thing from his mind.

What causes a man to risk his life in a far-off battlefield, especially when he is not compelled to do so? What caused David Sandler, in the face of German fire, to jump up and call to his men, "Let's get 'em," only to be shot in the head the next instant? Or Ralph White, with German soldiers within feet of him, to leap onto a tank and fire a machine gun against the brick house, triggering the almost certain German response in the form of a grenade, which exploded in front of him, flinging him into my arms badly wounded? Or the unknown (to me) soldier to be the first to get up and lead the charge on the brick house in the face of persistent enemy fire? Or Bill Devitt to leave the relative safety of a foxhole to drag his hysterical fellow soldier away from the exploding mortar shells back into the hole?

I can only speculate on the answer, especially as it applies to Bill Devitt. If this seems as though I'm blowing my own horn, I plead guilty, but I don't know how else to tell this. All sorts of reasons drive men to do such things, including *esprit de corps*, patriotism, peer pressure, fear of failure or retribution, responding to what they learned in training, instinctive reactions, compassion for others (including the feeling of comradeship with buddies), and a sense of duty.

Of these reasons, why I acted in a manner that could be characterized as "brave," I think the one which applied most often to me was my sense of duty. Although I've never tried to analyze before now why I acted as I did, I think it was usually this sense of duty, my feeling that I should do what was expected of me, which drove me.

When I dragged the hysterical man to the foxhole and when I left a hole to help the two badly wounded men, and at perhaps other times, I don't think that *esprit de corps* or patriotism moved me. My love and respect for E Company or the U.S.A. did not propel me out of those foxholes into the unprotected areas where I was risking my neck. But my feeling that this was something I should do, duty, got me going. On the other hand, when I walked into the cloud of black smoke and found Futch dead and Kurek badly wounded and then carried Kurek back to a dugout to protect him from further shellfire, I believe I was behaving largely in an unthinking, instinctive, reactive manner, for I was in the aftermath of a terrible explosion and I had to do something. But when I left the safety of my foxhole during an artillery barrage to comfort a man in another hole, I was probably motivated by a number of things —esprit de corps, compassion, peer pressure, fear of failure, responding to my training, as well as a sense of duty.

If someone years ago had discovered how to motivate soldiers to face death and mutilation in battle without flinching or holding back, the battles, and the history of the world, might have been very different.

More of the Ardennes

We spent the night of January 2, 1945, in a bivouac area in the Ardennes Forest, only a few miles behind the front lines. We dug holes in which to sleep, for warmth rather than for protection against enemy fire. I remember lining the bottom of my hole with pine needles, which were a handy substitute for a mattress.

Although the weather was cold, we were dressed for it. We each wore long winter underwear, olive drab woolen trousers and shirt, green cotton fatigue shirt and pants, a woolen sweater, a field jacket, and a woolen overcoat. We also wore around our waists a cartridge belt made of heavy webbed cotton held up by suspenders. We each wore one or two pairs of heavy socks, high top leather shoes, and black buckled overshoes. Over our lower pants legs were canvas leggings, which were laced in place. We had a woolen cap with a visor to fit under the helmet, and over the cap, the steel helmet. Finally, woolen gloves protected our hands. We must have appeared like a bunch of first graders all bundled up by our mothers to face a long walk to school on a cold winter day.

The Ardennes was heavily wooded, with many tall pines. It was memorable especially for the deep ravines that cut through the area. The roads meandered along the sides of the ravines so that while walking along a road we had high ground on one side and lower ground on the other with trees towering above us on both sides.

On the morning of January 3, the company left the bivouac area and started to move to the front. We trucked to within a mile or two of the front and then walked from there.

We were walking on a narrow gravel road. At first we could hear the familiar rumble of artillery and mortar fire ahead of us. Then, as though someone knew we were coming, some shells started to drop fairly close by. The company was walking in two columns, one on either side of the road. The temperature was about twenty-five degrees Fahrenheit, and a light snow was beginning to fall, but the ground did not yet have a blanket of snow on it. The heavy clothing I had on was good protection from the cold. Besides, we had been walking, so this kept us warm.

As we got closer to the front, we could hear more incoming artillery shells going over our heads, and we heard their explosions on all sides of us. Up until then, nothing landed close enough to hit anyone in the company. Sometimes, when the whistle of a shell would sound as if it were coming close to us, some of the men would stop and crouch down. Others would hit the deck. Since I thought I had developed a good ear for detecting incoming fire, I just kept walking. Such cockiness did not indicate that I was using good judgement, because I only had to be wrong once, and if a shell landed nearer than I thought it would, the results could have been fatal. On the other hand, such bravado, or pseudo-bravado, might have had

A view of the Ardennes Forest (left), showing how we were dressed but with more snow than when I was there. January 1945. (Photo courtesy of the 83rd Infantry Division Association)

A Town in the Ardennes (below), showing men wearing white camouflage jackets. We had not been issued such jackets when I was there. January 1945. (Photo courtesy of the 83rd Infantry Division Association)

a comforting or stabilizing effect on the men in the company. But I'm sure that I did no such philosophizing at the time.

Only artillery could be heard coming in. It made a whistling noise. Mortar shells would land without making a sound before they hit. But if we were close enough to the front we might hear the "bang," like a shot from a rifle, as the mortar shell was discharged from the tube from which it had been fired behind the enemy lines. But from the bang we could not determine whether the mortar shell would land near us or not.

Packer and I were walking along together. Up until then neither of us had stopped because of fear of the incoming fire. Suddenly, the whistle of an artillery shell announced a nearby explosion soon. Packer hit the ground. The shell went over our heads and exploded harmlessly. I stood there and watched Packer get up, and I teased him about hitting the ground unnecessarily. "What were ya doing, taking a break?"

He looked at me in silence while shaking his head, probably thinking, "What's that dumb bastard trying to prove?"

I didn't have much fear of the fire that was coming in around us. I had become accustomed to it, and did not really become frightened until it was close enough to cause casualties. The situation might be compared to that of iron workers who work thirty or more stories up on a skyscraper during its construction, yet are not greatly frightened by the height and the prospect of falling.

It was about three o'clock in the afternoon when we arrived at our position at the front. There is no sign with balloons stating, "This is the Front." There are other ways of finding out. The incoming fire became heavier, and we were told not to go beyond a ridge ahead of us.

We were to take positions along a low, treeless ridge beyond which there was an open valley and more forest beyond that. The Germans were in the forest.

The weather was getting colder. The snow was coming down harder, and there was a light dusting of it on the ground. We did not go to the top of the ridge because the Germans could have seen us. Instead we stayed on the reverse slope. As soon as we arrived, everyone started to dig slit trenches for themselves. Apparently the Germans did not know that we were on the ridge, since their artillery and mortar fire was falling a few hundred yards to our rear. The realization that the German fire could come closer at any time was sufficient incentive for us to dig as quickly as possible.

Every man carried on his rifle belt an entrenching tool that looked like a short-handled shovel. The head of the shovel could be folded back over the handle, making it shorter for carrying on the rifle belt. If the head of the shovel were adjusted at a right angle with the handle, then it could be used as a pick. In that position we could swing it and break into the frozen ground. Unfortunately, the ground was frozen so solidly that the digging was very slow. The slit trench I was digging was probably six feet long and two feet wide. I spent about two hours digging and only reached about six inches deep. It was like trying to dig into a block of ice.

Some brilliant planners had foreseen our digging problems. We had been issued small blocks of dynamite, which could be placed on the frozen ground at the location of the intended slit trench. After detonating the dynamite, "Voila", we would have our hole in seconds, instead of hours. None of the men in the company used the dynamite. Personally, I was afraid of all explosives and feared that I might have an accident. Besides, if we had started exploding the dynamite blocks so close to the German positions, they would have become aware of our location and directed their fire at us. What seemed like a good idea in theory didn't work out, at least in this situation.

As soon as it got dark, Packer and my new platoon sergeant and I went to the top of the ridge to see what faced us. This is called an "estimate of the situation," namely, an inspection of the area to see the intricacies of the terrain and the location of the opposing forces, with an eye to determine what action to take.

When we got to the top of the ridge, the German artillery and mortar fire was falling within 100 to 200 yards of us. As a precaution, I stood in an old German slit trench that was two or three feet deep. I figured that a little protection was better than none.

In the dim light we could see that the ridge sloped down to a valley, all of which was open ground. Halfway up the other side of the valley the bare ground became heavily wooded. The Germans were in the woods. The distance from the top of the ridge, where we were standing, to the edge of the woods, where the Germans were located, was only two to three hundred yards.

Packer, the platoon sergeant, and I talked quietly for a few minutes. Packer said, "The Krauts are in those trees. But if we're to get at them tomorrow, we can't go over the top of this ridge. So before it gets light in the morning, the three of us will have to scout around and find a way to attack without going over the ridge. I'll have the first sergeant call us a half hour before daylight."

"Are we going to attack first thing in the morning?" I asked.

"I don't know," Packer replied. "I'm to report to Colonel Norris in a little while, and he'll tell me."

"If we are," I said, "We'll want to get up earlier than that. We'll have to start the attack before daylight, so we'll need a good hour and a half to scout and eat and give the orders. I think we should go down now and see if we can find a way around this ridge so we won't take the time in the morning."

"I agree," said the sergeant. "We'll have plenty to do in the morning orienting the squad leaders and the other platoons."

"Okay. When we finish here, we'll go down and see if we can find a way," said Packer.

Although the German artillery and mortar fire was close, we didn't think we were in immediate danger. We had the problem of when and how we would attack the German positions the next day. Of course we knew generally where the Germans were—in the woods—but we had not as yet even seen a German. We also had the usual problems—feeding a large group of men and protecting ourselves against incoming fire.

But in war, as in ordinary times, it's funny how quickly one's plans can change.

Without warning, there was a large explosion. The war was over for me.

About thirty feet from where we were standing, a German mortar shell exploded with a flash of light and a big bang. The entire ridge was brightened momentarily by the flash. I immediately felt a sharp pain in my stomach. The platoon sergeant fell to the ground badly wounded. Packer said that he was hit slightly, and I slumped down into the hole to protect myself against any further explosions.

After being hit, my first reaction was fear. I was afraid I was going to die! Out in the middle of nowhere, and with a newly deposited piece of shrapnel in my stomach, fear was a natural reaction. Concurrent with the fear came a prayer, something like, "God help me." But simultaneously I started to talk to myself. "Don't panic. Seek help."

I called out *sotto voce*, "Medic, medic, I'm hit. Help me."

From a few feet to my right, I heard a voice, "Lieutenant, I'm the new medic. I'm here with the sergeant, but I can't find my damn flashlight. It's so damn dark, I can't see a damn thing. But we've gotta get help for him. He must be hit bad. I'll come as soon as I can."

"Okay," I said. "I'll be here."

Just then, I heard the sergeant groan, so I knew he was alive. Packer said to someone behind the hill, "Get two litters up here right away. Use a flashlight if you have to, but shut it off when you get up here. And hurry, Goddamnit. Hurry."

After a pause, Packer leaned over me and said, "How ya doing, Bill?"

"Okay, Bob. But get those litters up here."

As I lay in the hole I thought of trying to get up. Besides the great pain that I felt, I didn't know the extent of my injury and was afraid that if I tried to move I might make the wound more serious. So I lay as still as possible. As I lay there, I realized that my left hand was numb. I later learned that a piece of shrapnel had hit my left ring finger, sliced through my middle finger, continued into my hand between the middle and index fingers, and came to rest in the palm of my hand half an inch below the index finger.

The medic was a new man. This was his first time in combat, and there he was in the pitch black with three wounded men, two of whom, the sergeant and myself, were in bad shape. I have wished for years that I had said something to that young man to comfort and reassure him, such as "You're doing fine—take care of the others first." But I didn't. That noble thought rushed in after it was too late to act on it.

I had always thought that the reason the German mortar shell exploded near us so soon after we had got to the top of the ridge is that the Germans had seen us. We had made the mistake, I thought, of going to the top of the ridge before it was dark enough to conceal our presence. I had felt that I was, therefore, partially to blame for my wounds.

I've now changed my mind. I now realize that the Germans did not follow up the round that hit us with more rounds on our position. If they had known we were on the ridge, they would have plastered the area with mortar and artillery fire, and they didn't. My revised conclusion is that it was a short round that hit us and that we did not reveal our position when we went to the top of the hill.

The platoon sergeant was evacuated about when I was. I don't know whether he lived or died. I never saw him again. Packer was not evacuated, and spent the remainder of the war as commander of E Company.

Within ten minutes after I was hit, I was taken away on a stretcher. During that time, I'm sure that I did plenty of praying as well as hoping that the Germans would not follow up with more fire on our position.

They lifted me out of the hole onto the stretcher, and I was carried to the bottom of the ridge and put on a jeep that was modified to transport litters for the wounded. Although the ride was slow and bumpy, the trip back to the battalion aid station strapped to a litter on the back of an open jeep was uneventful. I was so busy worrying about my wounds that I don't remember the sergeant's being with me on the Jeep, but he must have been.

The battalion aid station was in a building a safe distance behind the lines. It provided emergency aid to the wounded before they were sent to a hospital for more treatment.

The doctor at the aid station put a bandage on my stomach wound, which was located about two inches above my navel. Although I didn't see it at the time, the wound was the shape of a quarter, perhaps a little larger. My stomach felt as though someone were sticking a razor sharp knife into it, again and again.

I was about to be taken off the examination table when I asked the doctor to look at my hand which, surprisingly, no one had noticed. I thought that one or two of the fingers were almost severed. I still had no feeling in the hand. Perhaps strangely, I wasn't concerned about whether or not I would lose a finger or two. I suppose I thought that ten fingers are more than anyone needs anyway. I was more concerned with the stomach wound, which was still causing intense pain. Nevertheless, I thought the hand, which was leaking blood from the three wounds on it, should be looked at.

"What about my hand, Doctor?" I said.

"Sorry, son," he said. "I didn't notice it. I'll just wrap it up, and they'll take care of it at the hospital."

The doctor sprinkled sulpha all over my bloody hand and put a bandage around the fingers and sent me off on a stretcher in an ambulance to the hospital.

Since the roads were snowy and icy, the ride back to the hospital was one of the more dangerous experiences that I had that day. We had heard that several ambulances had skidded off the roads into ditches, and that one had slid into a river. Although our ambulance did some slipping and sliding, we arrived safely at the hospital.

The Ardennes, showing a man on a litter on the back of a jeep. I could have posed for this picture on January 3, 1945. (Courtesy of the 83rd Infantry Division Association)

Chapter Nine

The End of the War in Europe
January 1945 to May 1945

The Hospital in Belgium

THE HOSPITAL, NOT SURPRISINGLY, was a Belgian one being used by the American army. I was carried into the lobby, where a great many men were lying on litters on the floor. While I lay there, a Catholic chaplain, a priest, came to me and asked, "How are you, Lieutenant? I'm Father Lundy. Are you Catholic?"

"Yes, I am, Father. Oh, I've felt better, but it's a lot better in here than up on the hill."

"I'll bet it is. Would you like me to give you Extreme Unction? Don't worry, just because we give the last rites of the Church doesn't mean you're going to die. I'm sure you'll be okay. But as long as the Church offers the sacrament of Extreme Unction at a time like this, you should take advantage of it."

"Oh, that's fine, Father. Go ahead."

The chaplain then proceeded to administer the sacrament, which consisted of the recitation of certain prayers and applying of specially blessed holy oils. After he finished, I said, "Father, I have a brother, Jim Devitt. He's a captain with the 45th Replacement Battalion. I think they're around here somewhere. Could you get hold of him and let him know I'm here?"

"Sure, Lieutenant. I'll be glad to, but I can't guarantee anything. With the units moving around so much, it might be impossible to find him. But I'll do the best I can."

"Thanks, Father. I understand."

"You're welcome, son. Goodbye and God bless you."

Jim was three years older than I. He also graduated from St. Thomas and received a second lieutenant's commission in 1942. He, too, was an infantry officer, but instead of being in a combat unit, he had been assigned, while in the States, to a replacement battalion. This was a unit that stayed behind the lines and fed and housed men who were moving up to the front to replace men who killed or wounded in combat. I don't know how or why Jim was lucky enough to have been assigned to a non-combat unit. Perhaps he had something which I, and my fellow infantry lieutenants, did not possess. After the war, Jim was Phi Beta Kappa, a Harvard Law alumnus, on the Board of Directors of Hart, Schaeffner, & Marx and several other large corporations, as well as president and chairman of a major New York insurance company. Maybe it was not all luck.

Soon after the chaplain left, I was taken to the operating room, where they put me to sleep, removed the shrapnel from my stomach, and sewed up my hand. I didn't lose a finger.

After I woke up, I was told that the doctors not only removed the piece of shrapnel from my stomach, but also pieces of clothing. The shrapnel had penetrated the anterior (outside) portion of my liver. I was told that if it had gone further into my liver I would have bled to death. Think back to all the clothing I was wearing, including the cartridge belt around my waist. The clothing undoubtedly reduced the impact of the shrapnel and probably saved my life.

The Map

When in combat, each officer usually was issued a map of the area where he was located. The map was folded and carried in a clear plastic case about three or four inches wide and several inches high. I carried mine in the large upper left pocket of my fatigue shirt. Soon after arriving in the hospital, I was taken to the operating room where a doctor examined me. My overcoat, field jacket, and sweater had been removed, so the

My brother, Captain Jim Devitt, who was stationed in the Ardennes only forty miles from the Belgian hospital in which I had my operation for my wounds. Jim visited me the next day, January 4, 1945. (Photo by author)

fatigue shirt was on the outside, and the map was clearly visible sticking out of the pocket.

When the doctor came to the table to examine me, he saw the map and asked me if he could have it. He said, "Well, Lieutenant, you won't need this again. Would you mind if I took it?"

What happened to the map was probably the least of my concerns, so I said, "Sure, Doctor, take it. It's no good to me anymore."

Besides, here was the fellow who was going to be cutting into me in the next few minutes, so this was no time to be chintzy about giving a map away.

I had had many maps in the past, and had discarded them when I left the area covered by the map, so I didn't care what happened to this one. But now, fifty years later, I wish that I had kept it, because I still don't know where in Belgium I was wounded. If I had that map today, perhaps I could find the spot.

The Visits

The day after the operation I lay in bed, hooked up to one tube that went from my mouth down my throat into my stomach, a second tube feeding blood plasma into one of my arms, and a third running a bottle of intravenous feeding material into the other arm. I felt pretty uncomfortable with all the machinery stuck into me, yet I wasn't in much pain, and I was happy to be clean and warm, and especially, safe.

Then, in walked Captain James Devitt. The chaplain had done his job! He had found my brother's unit, which was only forty miles away from the hospital. Seeing Jim was like getting a letter from home and simultaneously sitting down to Christmas dinner with my family. I don't know what we said to each other, especially since I couldn't talk well with the tube in my throat. But I'm sure that I felt I was the luckiest fellow in the hospital.

The next day Jim returned with two friends from his unit, Lieutenant "Curly" Schneideman and Captain "Mac"

Brothers, Lieutenant William L. Devitt and Captain
James E. Devitt, in the Place de la Concorde in "gay
Paree" after the war had ended in 1945. (Photo by
author)

McGuire. They gave me a giant Hershey bar with nuts (a hard item to get at that time), and since I couldn't eat anything, and they knew it, Curly said with a grin, "Gee, Bill, it's a shame you can't eat any of this. But I'll tell you, since you can't eat it, we'll help you out and eat some now so you won't be tempted to eat too much later on. We know it's bad for you."

Almost before I could reply, the three of them polished off the bar with much, much laughter, relieving me of any possible concern about the candy bar affecting my health. We talked and joked and ate the candy (most of us), and although we were in a large ward with dozens of men in their beds, we had a party as though no one else were present.

"We Regret"

Soon after Jim left, I wrote my mother and father to tell them that I was all right. I knew that Jim would write and that the War Department would notify them of my injuries. There was a special fast kind of mail service, called V-mail, which was said to guarantee speedy delivery. V-mail consisted of one page, about three by five inches in size, upon which the writer wrote his message. The page was then micro-filmed by the post office and airmailed to the United States, where the micro-film was enlarged to the original size of the letter and delivered to the addressee. I hoped that by getting a letter to my parents in my own handwriting before they received the official notification from the War Department, they would be relieved of much of the worry, uncertainty and anguish they would surely feel if the first information they received was a terse message from the Army.

The War Department won the race. Just a few days after I was wounded, a telegram from the War Department was delivered to Mr. and Mrs. Louis J. Devitt, 1736 Ashland Avenue, Saint Paul, Minnesota, stating, "We regret to inform you that your son, William, was seriously wounded in action on January 3, 1945."

I don't think that I ever discussed with my parents what their immediate reaction was when they heard the news, but

This is a copy of my first letter (V-Mail) home after I was wounded on January 3, 1945. The letter states that I was writing a week after the wounding. The text indicates writing only a day after, "Soon after Jim left, I wrote . . ." I must concede that my memory a week later must be better than after fifty-six years. Therefore, if anyone cares, the letter is correct. (Author's collection)

4196 U.S. Army Hospital Plant,
407
APO
New York. , % POSTMASTER
N.Y.

DEAR Mr. Devitt :

I am pleased to inform you that on 16 March 1945 your
(Date)

son , 1st Lt. William L. Devitt, O-518215
(Relationship) (Grade, name, Army serial number)

was* making normal improvement.

Diagnosis† Pentrating wound abdomen

* Enter present status as—
Making normal improvement.
Convalescing.
† Must be written in nontechnical
language.

W. D., A. G. O. Form 234
9 November 1944

Very truly yours,

Irving C. Pollock

IRVING C. POLLOCK, 1st Lt., MAC, Registrar.

16—42109-1 GPO

IF UNDELIVERED RETURN TO
CASUALTY BRANCH
THE ADJUTANT GENERAL'S OFFICE
WAR DEPARTMENT
WASHINGTON 25, D. C.

OFFICIAL BUSINESS

WASHINGTON, D.C. 21
MAR 22
7 - PM
1945

PENALTY FOR PRIVATE USE TO AVOID
PAYMENT OF POSTAGE $300
(GPO)

Mr. Louis J. Devitt
1736 Ashland Ave.
St. Paul. Minn.

This is the front and back of a postcard my parents received on March 26, 1945, from the War Department as to the state of my health on March 16, 1945. I can't locate the "seriously wounded" telegram they accepted in January. I'm sure the postcard was much more comforting to them than that terse telegram. (Author's collection)

I'm sure that there were plenty of tears, especially from my mother and sister, Mary, and perhaps also from my brother, Bob, who was only fourteen at the time, and a freshman at Saint Thomas.

After the tears, my dear Irish (second generation) Catholic mother determined to do what she could do for her boy, Billy, and that was to pray. She called her friends to ask them to pray for my recovery. In addition, she stepped up her usual recitation of the rosary, so that she was praying for me many times each day.

But that was not all. Within hours after receiving the telegram, my mother telephoned Father Vincent Flynn, president of Saint Thomas Military Academy. It was a Saturday, so Father Flynn invited my parents and Mary and Bob to a Mass to be offered for my recovery the next day in the chapel of Saint Thomas. They, of course, attended.

In the bed to my right lay a soldier who had been severely wounded and had tubes stuck in him similar to those in me. He was in great pain and kept calling to the nurses for help. I didn't even talk to him, and I don't know if he was rational. The nurses, I am sure, gave him morphine shots from time to time during the day, but he continued to complain. They tried to comfort him, and on one occasion I heard a nurse say, "Can't you be quiet like Lieutenant Devitt? He's hurting, too."

The truth was that I had nothing to complain about. I was having very little pain, and the doctors and nurses attended to all my needs. The admonishment from the nurses did not diminish his complaints, which continued into the night. I eventually fell asleep, and slept soundly until early the next morning, when I was awakened by a nurse. I saw that my neighbor's bed was empty, so I asked her, "Where'd he go?"

"Oh, I'm sorry, Lieutenant. He died during the night, and they took him away."

Paris

After a week or so, I was deemed well enough to be moved to the rear. Early one morning, I, together with other men, was placed in an ambulance to take us to a hospital in Paris. I was lying on my back on a stretcher facing the rear. It was a long journey and I fell asleep from time to time. Early in the evening, as I was napping, I was awakened suddenly by the pounding of the wheels on a cobblestone street. I wondered where we were, and from my position I could see out of the two rear windows, which were shaped like footballs standing on end. Through one window, appearing as though it had been placed there in a picture frame, I saw the Arc de Triomphe! Here was one of the most famous landmarks in Paris, and one of the few I would recognize instantly. If I had planned it, I couldn't have designed a more memorable introduction to the city.

After a few days in the Paris hospital, I was put on a train for Cherbourg, a port city on the coast of the English Channel. I remember that the train was very cold and that icy water was dripping from the ceiling past my face as I lay on a litter. I was not the uncomplaining chap that the nurse in the earlier hospital had thought me to be, for I complained to the attending nurse about the lack of heat and was rewarded with another blanket.

Crossing the Channel to England

Upon reaching Cherbourg, we were carried onto an English hospital ship for passage across the Channel to England. The English Channel is known for its rough seas, especially in winter, and it lived up to its reputation. The sea was so rough that the sisters (the English term for nurses) had trouble walking, and some got seasick. They sometimes had to hold on to something solid to keep from falling down. I had been on the ocean a few times before but I had never become sufficiently seasick to part company with my dinner. The sea was extremely rough, and it caused the ship to roll so far that

I was afraid I would be thrown out of my bunk. At the same time I was feeling sicker and sicker and realized that I was about to throw up. The next thing I knew, we were in the port of Southampton, being awakened for debarkation. I had fallen asleep and slept through the remainder of my battle with the English Channel.

It had been five months since I had left the English shores to take on the Germans. Thankfully, this was my last battle of the war.

The Hospital in Wales

From Southampton, we were taken to a hospital in northern Wales. Before many days had elapsed, I was allowed to get out of bed and walk. Although I was glad to be up, I found that walking was difficult. Having been in bed for the last few weeks, I was so weak at first that I had trouble standing. But what was worse, I was bent over like an old man crippled with age. I had an eight-inch cut down the right side of my belly, from which the shrapnel had been removed. The scar tissue rebelled when I tried to stand up straight, so for several days I walked like an old man.

But I developed a somewhat opposite problem with my left hand. I had trouble bending the fingers of my left hand, so I was sent to the X-ray department, where they found the small piece of shrapnel about three-fourths inch long and one-eighth inch square in the palm about a half inch below the left index finger. This was preventing me from bending my fingers, so, one morning I was taken to the operating room for removal of the shrapnel. The doctor put a local anesthetic into the hand and proceeded to remove the piece of German iron. Although I could have watched the operation, I looked away, since I didn't (and still don't) have any stomach for observing someone cut into me—or anyone else.

The operation was a success. I can now clench my left fist almost as tightly as my right. Except for the scars, the most memorable result of the wound is that one side of my left middle finger remains numb.

This is a copy of my V-mail letter of February 28, 1945 telling my family of the removal of a tiny piece of shrapnel from my hand. Also the envelope it came in. My mother printed "3/10/45" on the envelope, showing the date received. A bit slower than today's E-mail or Fax, but not bad with a war going on. (Author's collection)

There was little to do in the hospital but read, play poker, write letters and wait for mail from home. Because of my frequent moves after being hospitalized, it was some time before I received any mail.

The Lieutenant

One day a young lieutenant was brought into our ward. He had lost a leg in battle and was very upset and even despondent over his condition. After he had been there a few days, while walking past his bed, I detected a peculiar odor, like something rotting. I asked some of the other fellows in the ward whether they smelled this, and they replied that they had. The odor seemed to get worse each day, as did the state of the lieutenant's mind and health. He said he did not want to live as a cripple with only one leg.

As I was walking by him one day, I said, "How ya doing?"

"Not so good," he said. "This is terrible. Sometimes at night, I wake up from the pain in my foot and reach down to scratch it, and it's not there. I tell ya, I don't want to live like this. I think it's infected, and I don't give a damn. I wish it was over."

"I'm sorry," I said. "You know this'll be the worst part. After they get the infection cleared up, they can do wonders for ya. They get all you fellows walking again and I'll bet even running. I suppose that's easy for me to say, but don't give up."

"I really don't give a Goddamn anymore. How'll I play tennis? I had a football scholarship from Texas Christian waiting for me. I just don't want to live this way."

"I'll bet you'll play tennis again. Just don't give up."

"Don't give me that optimistic bullshit! Why don't ya go away. Go away, damnit!"

"I'm sorry. I didn't mean anything. I'll see ya later."

I left him and that was the last time we talked at any length.

After a few days, he was taken out of the ward and brought to a private room. Several days later we learned that he had died of gangrene. The lieutenant got his wish.

The Hospital in England

After I had recovered sufficiently to be ambulatory, I was sent to a hospital near Manchester where I spent the last two months of my hospitalization. While there, I learned that I had been promoted to First Lieutenant and had been awarded the Bronze Star medal. I was not thrilled. I'd hoped for the Silver Star. My ward housed about thirty young lieutenants, probably all of whom were battle casualties. We were all sick enough to be in the hospital but not so sick as to prevent us from seeking to stay amused at least fifteen hours a day. But playing poker and reading books all day and part of the night can get tedious.

The Countess

One break from the tedium was a weekly visit from a lady whom we called "the Countess." She was probably in her forties or fifties and talked with a foreign (not English) accent. Every week, she would come to our ward and visit the patients. She always brought cookies, cake, candy, or some combination of the three. This made her very popular, and we looked forward to the visits. One week the countess invited three of us to dinner the following Sunday. The plan was to take a bus into Manchester, meet the Countess' husband at the bus stop and then walk to their home.

Sunday arrived, and not one of us appeared at the bus stop. What happened?

To be succinct, we were a bunch of immature jerks. I think that my reason for not going was that I didn't feel like getting dressed up and taking a bus ride. The others had equally inane reasons for not showing up.

Although we had talked among ourselves prior to the designated Sunday about the prospective visit to the Countess' home, none of us had ever indicated to each other that he would not go. I think that I had planned to attend until the last minute, when lethargy overcame me. I thought when I decided to stay that the others would be going, and the others proba-

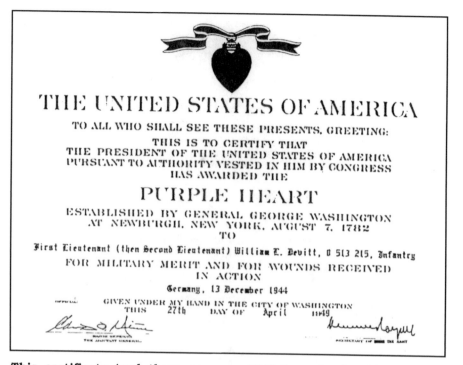

THE UNITED STATES OF AMERICA

TO ALL WHO SHALL SEE THESE PRESENTS, GREETING:

THIS IS TO CERTIFY THAT
THE PRESIDENT OF THE UNITED STATES OF AMERICA
PURSUANT TO AUTHORITY VESTED IN HIM BY CONGRESS
HAS AWARDED THE

PURPLE HEART

ESTABLISHED BY GENERAL GEORGE WASHINGTON
AT NEWBURGH, NEW YORK, AUGUST 7, 1782
TO

First Lieutenant (then Second Lieutenant) William C. Devitt, O 513 215, Infantry

FOR MILITARY MERIT AND FOR WOUNDS RECEIVED
IN ACTION

Germany, 13 December 1944

GIVEN UNDER MY HAND IN THE CITY OF WASHINGTON
THIS 27th DAY OF April 1949

This certificate (and those on page 184) I received evidencing my receipt of the Bronze Star Medal and the Purple Heart Medal with First Oak Leaf Cluster (meaning I received two Purple Hearts). Note the dates on which I earned the certificates, December 13 and 21, 1944, and January 3, 1945. For that three-week period, I seem to have acquired the knack of getting a medal each week. I was quite busy during that period. I figure that if I had kept as busy during my entire military career, I would have received about 100 medals, even more than Audie Murphy.

These certificates were found by me in the attic of my sister Mary's house in St. Paul. They were stored there with the affects of my parents after they had died. I don't remember ever receiving the certificates, although I have had the medals since 1945.

The Bronze Star was considered a sort of throw-away medal by some combat infantry men since it was also awarded to non-combat soldiers. The combat Bronze Star medal was given for heroic achievement while the non-combat one was for meritorious achievement. Thus a combat infantryman would get one for some heroic deed, but the medal looked the same no matter how it was earned. A cook might get a Bronze Star for baking the colonel's cake thirty days in a row without once having it fall, a meritorious achievement, something less praise worthy than the combat infantryman's deed, yet both men got the same medal.

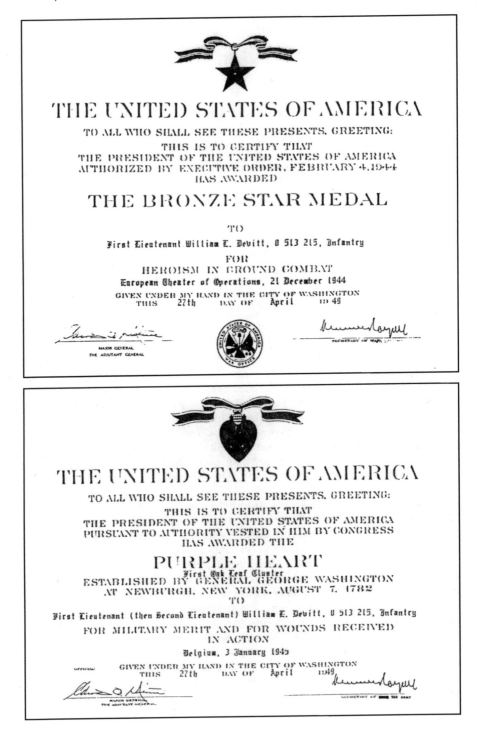

bly made the same assumption when they decided to absent themselves.

The Countess was not deterred by our rudeness from making her next weekly visit. At the time, she told us that her husband had waited for us at the bus stop for over an hour before realizing that nobody was coming. She said that she not only had a dinner waiting for us, but had invited some young ladies, who were disappointed at our failure to show. She, too, was very disappointed. I don't recall what explanation I gave the Countess for my rudeness, but I know that my deep shame was the only thing I deserved from the entire incident.

English Food

My only recollection of English food during the war came from the time I was offered an English biscuit by someone in the hospital, possibly the Countess. The biscuit looked to me like a round sugar cookie similar to those my mother used to make. But the similarity ended there.

As I bit into the biscuit, with visions of sugar cookies dancing in my head, I found in my mouth what seemed like a crispy piece of cardboard. Although I was hungry at the time, especially for something sweet, I don't think that I finished the small biscuit. I suppose that with the wartime shortages, the English were conserving sugar, but on that biscuit they carried conservation too far.

In April, the men in our ward heard that we would soon be ZIed. This meant we were to be sent back to the United States (the Zone of the Interior). We were all happy about this, and congratulated each other on our good fortune in not having to return to combat. When the orders came out, another man and myself were not ZIed, but instead received orders to return to our units, which were still fighting in Germany. All the other men in the ward were sent home.

FDR's Death

Upon being discharged from the hospital, I was given a one week leave in London prior to being returned to the 83rd Division. While I was there, President Franklin D. Roosevelt died in Warm Springs, Georgia, on April 12, 1945. A radio report from London stated the circumstances surrounding the President's death and added that all London had become quiet in mourning, and that even Piccadilly Circus, the entertainment center of London, was quiet.

What a lie! I had just come from Piccadilly Circus, and none of us had even heard of the death. The area was as noisy as ever, with the clear appearance of business as usual. From this incident, I learned to maintain a certain amount of skepticism in hearing or reading reports from the news media. I suppose that a quiet Piccadilly Circus made a good news story, but it lacked one essential ingredient—truth.

While on leave, I stayed in a London hotel with several Air Force pilots. One day I mentioned to them that I had a P-38 in my duffle bag somewhere in Europe. They all looked at me in disbelief. "What the hell are you talking about, Devitt?" one of them said.

I replied to him in a less-than-patient tone, "Look, I got the P-38 off a German prisoner. If you fellows were in the real war, you'd know that a lot of the Germans carry P-38s and Lugers."

On hearing the word "Lugers," the pilots realized that the P-38 I had in my duffle bag was a pistol and not the P-38 fighter plane, which they had pictured in their minds.

At the end of my leave, I joined a group of men who were to be returned to their units fighting in Germany. We were all combat veterans who did not look forward to rejoining our units, not because we didn't respect them, but because we were fearful of returning to combat.

In the first week of May, we sailed across the English Channel and landed in Le Havre, France, on the Normandy coast. In Le Havre, we boarded boxcars (called "40-and-8s" from the French phrase meaning forty men or eight horses) for the trip across France.

Although I was heading back to combat, I was not yet very worried about it. We knew from the papers that the war in Europe was coming to an end. Besides, my division, the 83rd, was one of the farthest advanced into Germany, so it would take longer for me to get there. Further, the war didn't ever seem real or threatening to me until I got close enough to the front to hear the rumble of artillery fire.

On the other hand, I realized that one day more of combat combined with some bad luck could have been fatal. I knew that I had come within a hair's breadth of dying in my one day of combat in Belgium. If that shrapnel had gone any further into my liver, I would have bled to death.

But my concern was unnecessary, for the war in Europe ended on May 8th, while my group of hospital returnees was in München-Gladbach, in western Germany, hundreds of miles from the front lines. Inexplicable as it might appear, the remaining soldiers, sailors, and flyers were able to finish off the Germans without my help.

Three months later the A-bombs were dropped, the Japanese surrendered, and the war was over.

If there is any single message I wish a reader take from this story, it is this: overwhelmingly, the greatest number of casualties suffered by the United States' Army in Europe during World War II was inflicted on a relatively small group— namely, the front-line infantrymen. They were the infantrymen who were constantly face to face with the enemy and lived with the ever-present risk of death or injury.

The front-line infantrymen whom I remember most deeply were those who were killed in action.

I still recall the incident in which I left my foxhole to help a soldier who was hit by a tree burst in the Hürtgen Forest. As I knelt over him, I was sickened by the odor of burning flesh caused by the red hot shrapnel in his chest. Minutes later, he died.

David Sandler was a fellow lieutenant whose platoon was pinned down by small arms fire. He called out, "Come on, let's get 'em!" He got up, and a German soldier promptly shot him through the head.

Finally, I can never forget Futch, who, without hesitation, obeyed my order of "Follow me" and ran closely behind me until a chunk of German shrapnel tore off the top of his head. If he had not obeyed immediately and instead had held back for only five seconds, he might be alive today.

The sacrifices of the front-line infantrymen, whether they died in battle or "only" risked their lives, were well summarized some 2,000 years ago by this biblical passage:

> "Greater love hath no man than this, that a man lay down his life for his friends."[13]

---

[13]Chapter 15, Verse 13, St. John's Gospel, *The King James Bible.*

Epilogue One

"Never in the field of human conflict was so much owed by so many to so few."[14]

I think that Churchill's tribute to the Royal Air Force quoted above could well be applied to the young men of the class of 1941 of St. Thomas Military Academy, and of E Company, 330th Infantry.

Graduates of ROTC schools, such as St. Thomas, also suffered a disproportionately high number of battle casualties. Out of a class of ninety-five in my 1941 graduating class at St. Thomas, some of whom did not serve in the armed forces, six of my classmates were killed in military service, and about thirty were wounded, many more than once. One of the six was killed in an Air Force training accident. The other five were infantrymen who died in combat. Therefore, about six percent were killed and thirty percent wounded.

Comparing these percentages to the percentages of casualties suffered by all men who served in the United States armed forces during the war,[15] the St. Thomas class of 1941

---

[14]Winston Churchill, tribute to the Royal Air Force, House of Commons, August 20, 1940.

[15]*The World Almanac Book of Facts - 1990* shows that during World War II, the United States Armed Forces suffered battle casualties of 292,131 deaths and 670,846 wounded out of a total of 16,353,659 who served. Thus, 1.78 percent were killed in action, and 4.1 percent were wounded.

suffered deaths at over three times the rate, and wounded at over seven times the rate, sustained by the armed forces in general.

From the time E Company entered the Hürtgen Forest on about December 3, 1944, until I was wounded in Belgium on January 3, 1945, the company suffered an estimated fifteen killed in action and 110 wounded. It started the campaign with about 190 men. Thus, for this period, the company suffered about eight percent killed and sixty percent wounded.

Again comparing these percentages to the percentage of casualties suffered by those who served in the United States armed forces, in this period the men of E Company suffered deaths at over four times and wounded at fourteen times the rates sustained by the armed forces in general during the war.

Epilogue Two

Observations Arising from a Visit to Europe in 1988

As to Chapter Two - Normandy

Omaha Beach Revisited

In July of 1988 my wife, Mary, and I made a trip to retrace my journey through Europe in 1944 and 1945. This was my first time back. I had told Mary of my landing on Omaha Beach and walking past a large concrete German bunker about halfway up the hill. The bunker has now been turned into a monument dedicated to the men who served in the United States National Guard during the war, many of whom were on Omaha Beach during the fighting there.

I was pleased to see the bunker in the location where my memory had placed it. I harkened back to my first visit to the beach and to my speculating as to how the attacking American soldiers were able to get past that formidable bunker. I still wonder how they accomplished this, while it was spewing a dense spray of deadly fire. Of course, many did not.

As to Chapter Three - Brittany

Ile de Cezembre, 1988

After Omaha Beach, Mary and I visited St. Malo. In 1944, I joined E Company in Dinard and never did go across the river (that separates Dinard and St. Malo) to St. Malo. In planning the trip, prior to leaving home, I had written in my itinerary "St. Malo" as one of the places to revisit without thinking that in the war I had actually been in Dinard and not St. Malo. My greatest interest in visiting St. Malo or Dinard was to see the Ile de Cezembre again. I had told Mary many times about our near attack of the island, so I, and I hope she, looked forward to seeing it.

In driving to St. Malo and Dinard from Omaha Beach, one comes first to St. Malo. We were there in late July, at the height of the tourist season. It is located on St. Malo Bay, with a long coastal roadway overlooking the Ile de Cezembre. Within St. Malo the road separates the city from the bay. On one side of the road is a seawall that protrudes about four feet above the road. On the other side are buildings housing antique shops, restaurants, and souvenir stores.

Mary and I got out of our car and looked over the sea wall in search of the Ile. There are several islands in the bay, but I soon recognized the Ile de Cezembre. This brought back forcefully the memories of our near attack and fortunate escape from heavy casualties on the Ile.

Soon after first seeing the Ile, we went into a souvenir store where I saw the proprietor, a gray-haired Frenchman about my age. I wanted to tell someone of my near brush with the Ile forty-four years before, so I chose the proprietor to be the victim. As soon as I started to relate the story, I, of course, referred to World War II. Upon mention of the word "war," the Frenchman turned on his heel and walked away from me, saying that he did not want to hear about it.

I was enraged by his reaction. Although I didn't expect the French to treat me like a conquering hero as they had during the war, I did feel that I should be treated in a civil manner. In my anger I started to walk toward the Frenchman, but Mary put her hand on my shoulder and told me to calm down. I didn't want to "calm down," but I knew she was right, so I did nothing further.

I couldn't stop thinking, "How soon they forget." It was "only" forty-four years before that the men of E Company were ready to give up their lives to retake that small island. To me the time seemed like hours rather than years since that band of young Americans prepared to go down to the boats to launch the attack. Yet that Frenchman, in refusing even to listen to my story, seemed to deny what had happened in 1944.

Since this incident took place, I have harbored a dislike for all of the French people. This is not rational, but I suppose that this is the kind of circumstance out of which prejudice arises.

As to Chapter Four - Luxembourg

Finding the Chateau

As Mary and I drove through Luxembourg, I didn't remember the names of the towns I'd been to in 1944. I had told Mary many times about the Chateau, but I wasn't sure that I could find it. After some searching we came upon a building that I thought was the Chateau. It looked like the right building and was located behind a high hill overlooking the Moselle River. However, I had a serious doubt that this was the Chateau because between the building and the hill was another building, which I did not recall having been there in 1944. Mary and I met and talked to the present owner of the Chateau (who had owned it only for the past few years), and he said that he thought that the "other" building had been there prior to 1944. It also looked old, so I agreed with him. I, therefore, left the area thinking that the building we had seen was not the Chateau.

Before leaving the area I took a picture of the Chateau with Mary and the owner in front of it. One evening after we had returned home from the trip, I was looking through some old photographs and discovered a snapshot of the Chateau taken when I was there in 1944. I'd forgot that I had it. I immediately got out the picture that we had taken a few weeks before. It was the Chateau! The two photographs appeared to have been taken from the same spot. I couldn't have taken the second picture from a better angle if I had had the first picture in front of me. As to the other building, it was probably there in 1944, and I simply did not recall it.

As to Chapter Six - Hürtgen Forest- Part Two

The Brick House - Again

I tried to take photographs of the places I had seen during the war. Just before we left home, we purchased a new camera, so I was unfamiliar with how it worked. Before arriving in Strass, I wondered if the town would have changed much from 1944. I was especially interested in seeing the brick house, and in finding out if the house and its surroundings were still intact. To my delight, the town and brick house were still there, and seemed much the same as they had been in 1944. Of course there was no rubble, but there were also no new three-bedroom frame ramblers such as one might find in an American town.

The brick house seemed the same, but it was surrounded by a wire fence with a sign at the front gate that warned, in German, "Beware of the Dog." I didn't see a dog, so I opened the gate and knocked at the front door. I hoped to get into the house and at least see the basement in which I had spent such eventful hours. But after repeated knocking, I realized that no one was home.

I was greatly disappointed in not getting into the house, but I still had the consolation of knowing that I could take some photographs. As I was thinking about the locations from which to take the pictures, I realized that I had just used up the roll of film in the camera, and would have to insert a new one. This was only about the third or fourth time that I had had occasion to change the film in the new camera. To the ordinary person this is no challenge, but to a mechanically inept soul such as I, this was a daunting experience. I failed. I couldn't get the film properly into the camera. Therefore, not only was I unable to photograph the brick house, but also I could take no pictures in Untermaubach, which I visited the same day.

As to Chapter Seven - Untermaubach

The same day that I revisited Strass in 1988, I went back to Untermaubach. This little town, in which I had spent three days in 1944, seemed much unchanged. While there, I learned that the place I had described as a church (which overlooked the Roer River and was the last building we took in the town) was actually a small monastery with a chapel that I had mistaken for a church. The village church is about twenty yards west of the monastery.

Soon after arriving in Untermaubach, I sought out and found the pastor of the church, who was a Catholic priest. In introducing myself to the pastor, I told him of my wartime experience in the town. He told me that he had served in the German army during the war and was taken prisoner by the French. He also confided that he had a sister living in Dallas, Texas, as well as another sister living in San Francisco. He offered to drive me into the Hürtgen Forest, but I reluctantly had to decline because my time schedule did not allow for it.

After a bottle of beer in the priest's house, I decided to leave a little monetary gift with the pastor and his parish. I looked in my pockets and saw that I only had three or four marks, which were worth no more than one or two American dollars. Although I'm a pretty penurious fellow, I, nevertheless, felt that twenty to twenty-five dollars would be a more appropriate amount.

The only other funds I had with me were travelers checks in $100 denominations. There was no bank in town, so there was no place to exchange travelers checks for marks. My dilemma was how to appear as generous as possible without disregarding my better judgement by giving what I considered a foolhardy amount. The dilemma was insoluble, so against my penny-pinching nature, I gave one of the $100 travelers checks to the pastor. I think that even he was surprised by the amount, for he asked me the purpose of the gift. I told him that since I had helped damage the Church's and town's property years before, I wanted to make a little repayment. I did not tell him that my apparent generosity was driven less by munificence than by the fear of appearing cheap (by giving only three or four marks).

Epilogue Three

Comparing the Period 1937 to 1945 with the Present

As to Chapter One - In the United States and England

During my years at St. Thomas I took the military training in stride and accepted as gospel everything that was taught. The training manuals supplied by the army contained all sorts of instructions on military tactics. For example a manual would explain how the scouts of a rifle platoon would precede the platoon out of a woods into an open field in an approach march formation prior to contact with the enemy. The manual would state, for example, that the scouts, upon seeing the enemy, would give the arm and hand signal for "enemy in sight." I never questioned this procedure while in school, but I now know that the scouts probably would have been fired on, and possibly hit, so there would have been no need for a signal to advise the others of the presence of the enemy. The manuals were rather sterile, unrealistic tomes that often failed to include the human, unpredictable element into combat situations. I realize this now, but I didn't in 1941.

As to Chapter Two - Normandy

As I said before, my thoughts about Omaha Beach are the same now as they were in 1944, namely how did the attacking Americans manage to get off the beach and to the higher ground in face of the deadly German fire? The answer is that those few who made it did so by means of great courage, skill, and resourcefulness. My old and good friend, Bob Huch, was an assault section leader in the first wave on D-Day with E Company, 16th Infantry, First Infantry Division (known as the Big Red One from the large, red numeral one on its shoulder patch). Bob and I were old schoolmates, having graduated together from St. Mark's Grade School in St. Paul and St. Thomas Military Academy, and after the war attended the University of Minnesota together. In 1991, I visited Bob at our St. Thomas' fiftieth reunion in Minneapolis. (Sadly, he died a few months prior to this writing). I told him that I was writing this story, so he later wrote to me about his experiences on D-Day. My combat experiences pale compared to his, for he was in a rifle company in North Africa, Sicily, D-Day, and through Europe to the end of the war. I'm almost ashamed to talk about myself when I think of how much more he went through. It's ironic that Bob Huch, who was perhaps one of the least military minded or shoe shining members of our St. Thomas class, probably spent more time as a front-line infantryman than any of the rest of us. The answer as to how the men on D-Day got on and off the beach is described in the following excerpts from a letter dated June 26, 1944, from Bob to his parents and a report of Captain Edward Wozenski, commander of E Company, 16th Infantry:

From Bob Huch's letter (see Appendix C for the full text):

". . . At about 800 yds. off shore the shelling and machine gun fire started—with the latter bouncing off the boat making quite a racket. Down went the ramp, and into five feet of water went me—followed by the section.

". . . All the way in thru the water, the bullets were splashing right in front of my nose, on both sides, and everywhere. Somehow I made it [ashore]—many people didn't. . . . it was about 400 yards to the high water mark, where there was a dune, about three feet high—the only cover after leaving the boat. The Jerry machine guns were sweeping the beach . . . I'd advance about 30 yards, and then hit the dirt, bullets going everywhere. Somehow I made the sea-wall, and was the first to make that spot . . . I'd look back and see the section trying to get in—and it was awful. People dying all over the place . . .

". . . I've never seen so many brave men who did so much—many would go way back and try to gather in the wounded and themselves get killed. . . . On the beach and shortly thereafter, I didn't observe one act of cowardice or hesitancy to respond to orders—not one . . ."

From Capt. Edward Wozenski's report (See Appendix D for the full text):

"Working their way up to the top of the high ground overlooking the beach, the 1st platoon, under covering fire from the rest of the company, worked west where the strong point was reduced—pillbox by pillbox. . . . Extremely stubborn resistance was encountered in this strong point, with its maze of underground shelters, trenches, and dug-outs . . .

"Two skeleton sections of the company moved up under Lt. Robert A. Huch . . . The situation at the time was extremely touch and go, with the enemy in front, amongst, and behind us. Still Lt. Huch led his men into this rather desperate situation where, by setting himself up and holding his ground, he eased the dangerous pressure on "G" company's right. . . . Though completely surrounded many times, knowing that no supporting troops were nearby, and without communications of any kind, the company held this ground throughout the critical night . . ."

In order to put into historical perspective Bob Huch's actions on D-Day, he was one of the few leaders of the first wave of (in my estimation) the most important military action by United States forces in World War II.

According to Bob, the D-Day casualties of E Company, 16th Infantry were 112 killed and twenty-seven wounded out of 183 men in the company. Of those who were killed, many had been wounded but later were killed on the beach by German mortar and machine gun fire while waiting to be evacuated. Of the 183 men (176 enlisted men and seven officers), forty-two enlisted men and two officers remained at the end of the twenty-four-hour period following the landing.

E Company, 16th Infantry probably suffered more killed in action on D-Day than were suffered by my company, E Company, 330th Infantry, during its several months of combat, and we weren't a bunch of skedaddlers.

As to Chapter Three - Brittany

(a) Although I still wonder how Bonnet felt in giving up command of the platoon to me, I don't think that I ever could have asked him how he felt. He might have said that he wanted to leave the army for good when he realized he was being replaced by a skinny young fellow with glasses with few, if any, outward attributes of a leader and zero combat experience.

(b) Also, it certainly doesn't take a genius to realize that one should not sneak into a mess tent to steal food, especially an officer. But I don't think that this occurred to me until recently. Perhaps this is proof that I'm a bit below genius.

As to Chapters Five, Six, and Seven - Hürtgen Forest Parts 1 and 2 and Untermaubach

(a) If I were to replay the scene of the two badly wounded men caught in the open, I would have insisted that three or four of my men get out of their holes to help. They could have given first aid to the man lying against the tree and helped carry both men out. Today I don't understand why I didn't call any of my men to help. As a leader one of my main jobs was to tell my people what to do, to give orders, but in this situation I guess I forgot about that.

(b) I wish that I could thank Marty Martinson again and more completely for his kindness in saving his gum for me. I realize now more than in 1944 the great selflessness shown by Marty in thinking about me under such unbelievably adverse conditions. I've tried to find him but without success.

(c) In the "Attack in the Woods" my description gives the impression that the company was wandering around aimlessly while suffering casualties with no apparent objectives. I'm sure that we had received orders with specific objectives, but I just don't remember what they were or how well we accomplished them.

(d) Today would I have gone to the rescue of the men in the knocked out tank? I don't think so. If some of us had tried to cross the open field to get to the tank, German small arms' fire might have caught us out in the open with disastrous results. We probably considered this possibility at the time and decided not to risk the loss of more men with such an uncertain prospect of success. After a soldier has been in combat a while, he becomes very pragmatic and increasingly more cautious. Soldiers tend to take fewer chances and find ways to avoid unnecessary risks. Some men, as they survived more and more combat, felt that their time was sure to come at any moment. They became unduly fearful and, therefore, ineffective and unable to take the necessary risks that are an essential element in carrying out one's duties as a combat infantryman. Fortunately, I never experienced the feeling.

(e) I regret today that we never sang while we marched. Singing is good for morale and makes time go faster while marching. It certainly would have made a dramatic ending to these chapters if I could honestly have related that as the little group of survivors from E Company walked out of Untermaubach, they had broken into "God Bless America" or possibly (but improbably) "Deutschland Über Alles."

As to Chapter Eight - Belgium - The Battle of the Bulge

(a) Eisenhower and Bradley were two of the most respected American generals. Bradley was even called the

"Soldier's General," or something similar. Neither, however, had ever led a rifle platoon or a rifle company in combat. As junior officers, they had probably led troops in training exercises, and when they were older they might have taught infantry tactics at Fort Benning or elsewhere. But without experiencing it, they didn't have the foggiest notion of what it was like to be an infantryman in combat.

An infantryman's combat experience might be compared to a woman's experience in giving birth to a baby. As my wife has told me, a person really doesn't know what it's like without having experienced it. It's easy to take calculated risks when miscalculations will cause suffering to someone other than oneself, especially when one never has experienced similar suffering. I do not mean to imply that Eisenhower or Bradley were heartless, uncaring, or incompetent men. But I don't think that a person can make the best possible decision without knowing all the facts. And those American generals, in making their calculated risks that led to the Battle of the Bulge, didn't know all the facts—they had never been combat infantrymen.

It can be argued that the Duke of Wellington, Robert E. Lee, and Napoleon Bonaparte were all great generals yet they were never combat infantrymen. (I am aware that both Lee and Napoleon had certain combat experience before they became generals.) My answer is that war was very different from the days of those generals to the days of World War II. Wellington, Lee, and Napoleon lived in times when the armies fought pitched battles in a fairly limited area. And the weapons then did not have the range nor the destructive power of the weapons of World War II. At the battle of Waterloo, Wellington and Napoleon could view large parts of the battlefield at any one time without great personal risk, and Lee was able to order and observe Pickett's fateful charge at Gettysburg.

But in World War II, many high-ranking generals were pencil pushers—that is, they could give orders by marking positions on a map with pencils, often without seeing the terrain involved. In World War II, the battlefields were so vast that a general could only hope to see small parts of them. Besides, since the artillery, mortars, and air attacks caused a very high volume of fire to fall on the front lines, it was extremely risky to go up to the front where the fighting was taking place. If the generals had spent as much time at the front as the infantrymen, the armies would soon have run out of generals. Perhaps that would not have been all bad.

On further consideration of what I have just argued about the desirability of a general's having combat infantry experience, my argument may be something less than absolutely correct. First, there is little correlation between the skills needed to lead a rifle platoon and to command an army. A platoon leader might need the courage and skill necessary to lead his platoon in an assault in the face of enemy fire, but a general does not have the occasion to exercise such qualities.

Second, there is the practical question of how generals acquire combat infantry experience. Unless a general, earlier in his life, were just the right age to have a war come along so that he could have had the opportunity to lead a rifle platoon or rifle company, he could have had no such experience.

Third, if a general becomes overly concerned with the suffering endured by his men, he may not make the tough decisions sometimes required of the battlefield commander. War is not a football game. A battlefield commander must, in order to gain a military objective, give orders to his men that will lead to their death or injury. To hesitate or fail to give such orders out of compassion for his men may cause such commander's unit to fail in its objective as well as causing the failure of a larger unit of which his is a part.

Then there were the good old days, when the king led his men into battle. I don't know that Henry V was aided or hampered in his decision to take on the French at Agincourt[16] because of the fact that he would be in the middle of the bat-

---

[16]The Battle of Agincourt took place on October 25, 1415, near the town of Agincourt, France, and was between the English, led by the English King, Henry V, and the French, who outnumbered the English about five to one. The French had about 60,000 soldiers, while the English had 10,000 to 15,000. The battle resulted in an overwhelming victory for the English.

tlefield. But if Henry could fight with the adroitness that William Shakespeare gave him in speaking to his men just prior to Agincourt, no wonder the English won the battle.

> "This day is call'd the feast of Crispian:
> He that outlives this day, and comes safe home,
> Will stand a tip-toe when this day is named,
> And rouse him at the name of Crispian.
> He that shall live this day, and see old age,
> Will yearly on the vigil feast his neighbors,
> And say, 'Tomorrow is Saint Crispian'
> Then will he strip his sleeve and shew his scars,
> And say 'These wounds I had in Crispin's day.'
> . . .
> And Crispin Crispian shall ne'er go by,
> From this day to the ending of the world,
> But we in it shall be remembered;
> We few, we happy few, we band of brothers;
> For he today that sheds his blood for me
> Shall be my brother; be he ne'er so vile,
> This day shall gentle his condition:
> And gentlemen in England now a-bed
> Shall think themselves accursed they were not here,
> And hold their manhoods cheap whiles any speaks
> That fought with us upon Saint Crispin's day."
>
> William Shakespeare,
> The Life of King Henry V,
> Act IV, Scene 3

Another stirring speech came from Henry (as told by Shakespeare) about a month prior to Agincourt while he and his men were outside the town of Harfleur about to breach its walls after they had besieged the town for several weeks. The French surrendered the town without a fight.

> "Once more unto the breach, dear friends, once more;
> Or close the wall up with our English dead.
> In peace there's nothing so becomes a man
> As modest stillness and humility:

But when the blast of war blows in our ears,
Then imitate the action of the tiger;
Stiffen the sinews, summon up the blood,
. . .
Now set the teeth and stretch the nostril wide,
Hold hard the breath and bend up every spirit
To his full height. On, on, you noblest English,
. . .
Dishonor not your mothers; now attest
That those whom you call'd fathers did beget you.
Be copy now to men of grosser blood,
And teach them how to war. And you, good yeomen,
Whose limbs were made in England, show us here
The mettle of your pasture; let us swear
That you are worth your breeding; which I doubt not;
For there is none of you so mean and base,
That hath not noble luster in your eyes.
I see you stand like greyhounds in the slips,
Straining upon the start. The game's afoot:
Follow your spirit, and upon this charge
Cry 'God for Harry, England, and St. George!'"

William Shakespeare
The Life of King Henry V
Act III, Scene 1

In contrast I had neither the inclination nor the ability to exhort my men prior to an attack. I would simply give them as much information as I had and rely on them to do the best they could. Perhaps the army should have hired a few Shakespeares to compose stirring exhortations for the use of leaders.

(b) Would I fall asleep again if I had a second chance to take the truck ride? I hope not, but I'm afraid I might. There is nothing more comfy and soporific than being warm and dry when the snow is blowing against the window and you're tired and have been out in the cold. Since everyone in the other cabs managed to stay awake, I could have done something to remain alert such as talking or singing. Today I might take my responsibilities more seriously and concentrate on staying awake, but I must admit that I deserved to be tarred and feathered for my sleeping spell in the truck.

(c) I spent about two hours digging a slit trench six feet by two feet and about six inches deep. Having had fifty years to think about it, I might have made the hole half as long (three feet instead of six) but twice as deep (twelve inches instead of six), allowing me to curl up into it in the event of enemy fire. What I don't recall is whether or not two of us were digging the hole, so if the hole were two by three instead of two by six, one of us would have been left out in the open. Fifty years of thinking hasn't helped.

(d) If I had not been standing in the German slit trench when I was hit, I possibly would have been hit in the leg, undoubtedly a far less serious wound. But I also, by standing in the hole, probably avoided shrapnel that went over my head and which otherwise would have hit me. Having had a long time, unlike in 1945, to consider the various possibilities, I think I made the correct decision.

Chapter Nine - The End of the War in Europe

Of one thing I'm sure. Today I would certainly attend the Countess' dinner. No wonder that during the war the British and others sometimes considered the American soldier to be boorish, especially if our performances toward the Countess were used as the criterion of American behavior.

Appendix A

Bayonet Drill

This section is included at the suggestion of my youngest son, Willy, while recognizing the great probability of putting the reader to sleep with a description of bayonet drill, which is about as scintillating as watching grass grow. If you fall asleep, blame Willy.

The first order given by the instructor was "On Guard." At this command, a man would grasp the rifle (with the bayonet attached) at the grip (near the trigger) with the right hand, while the left hand held the stock under the barrel. He would stand facing the front, with his feet about a foot and a half apart with the knees slightly bent. The rifle was waist high and would be pointed to the front, as if to confront an adversary. On Guard was the beginning position for most bayonet exercises.

Another command was "Long Thrust and Hold," which followed "On Guard." At this command, a man would step forward with his left foot and thrust the rifle at arm's length toward the chest of the imaginary foe. The right hand held the rifle at the grip, with the right forearm resting on top of the rifle's butt, while the left hand held the stock. The rifle with the bayonet weighed close to ten pounds, so some instructors, to test the strength of their men (or perhaps for pure meanness) would order the men to remove their left hands, leaving the ten pounds to be held solely by the right hand and arm, which were toward the rear of the rifle. This was like holding a fishing pole with one hand while a ten pound walleye was on the line, but without the satisfaction of catching the fish. This command was not a popular one, and usually the length of time that the right hand and arm were so committed was not long. I abstained from use of this command, probably from fear that some disgruntled trainees with aching right arms might meet me some dark night on a deserted street.

The drill also included the use of the butt of the rifle as a sort of battering ram. On command, from the On Guard position, a man would step forward with his right foot and swing the butt upward with the right hand toward the chin of the imaginary foe. This maneuver would end up with the man holding the rifle upside down about shoulder-high with the butt pointed toward the front.

From this latter position, upon command, "Smash," the rifle butt was thrust forward parallel to the ground against the head of the now thoroughly battered foe.

I don't know whether these maneuvers were ever used in combat, but I think they were worthwhile in showing men that they had a way of defending themselves so long as they had their rifles and bayonets.

Appendix B

Infantry Division Organization

The T.O. (table of organization) called for a rifle company to have 187 enlisted men and six officers. The rifle company consisted of three rifle platoons, a weapons platoon, and company headquarters.

The rifle platoon consisted of a platoon leader (a first or second lieutenant), a platoon sergeant, second in command, (a technical sergeant, with three stripes up and two stripes below, located on the upper sleeve of both arms), a platoon guide, third in command, (a staff sergeant, three stripes up and one stripe below), a runner who was the platoon leader's radio man (a private or private first class, who wore one stripe) and three squads of twelve men each consisting of a squad leader (a sergeant—three stripes up), an assistant squad leader (a corporal—two stripes up) and ten other men (either privates or privates first class).

The weapons platoon consisted of a platoon leader (a first or second lieutenant), a platoon sergeant, a platoon guide, a mortar section, and a light machine gun section. The mortar section consisted of a section leader (staff sergeant) and three squads of about five men each. The light machine gun section had a section leader and two squads of about five men each.

The company headquarters consisted of the company commander, a captain, the executive officer, who was second in command, usually a first lieutenant, and first sergeant, the highest ranking enlisted man in the company, the company clerk, the mess sergeant and his kitchen personnel, the supply sergeant and his men, plus jeep drivers and other men.

Of the twelve men in a rifle squad, eleven were armed with the M-1 rifle (a .30-caliber, eight-shot, semi-automatic rifle) and the twelfth had an automatic rifle, usually called a BAR (Browning Automatic Rifle). A semi-automatic rifle is one that fires only one shot when the trigger is pulled but automatically cocks itself to fire another round. An automatic rifle is one that fires continuously as long as the trigger stays pulled. Obviously, the volume of fire that the rifle squad delivered (fire power) depended greatly on the BAR. Although not standard equipment, some men carried sub-machine guns (Thompson sub-machine gun—Tommy gun), the type of automatic weapon seen in the gangster movies, and some carried the M3 grease gun, an all metal automatic weapon, a somewhat smaller version of the Tommy gun. The company also had several bazookas, which fired anti-tank rockets.

There were three sixty millimeter mortars in the mortar section.

There were two light machine guns in the light machine gun section. These were .30-caliber automatic weapons fired from a bi-pod on the ground.

An infantry division consisted of about 11,000 men. It was composed of three infantry regiments of about 3,000 men each plus artillery, engineers, transportation, supply, medical, signal corps, and other supporting services.

The infantry regiment included three infantry battalions of approximately 1,000 men each plus supporting troops. Every infantry regiment consisted of companies A, B, and C, which were rifle companies, and D, a heavy-weapons company, all of which were in the First Battalion; companies E, F, and G, rifle companies, and H, a heavy-weapons company in the Second Battalion; and companies I, K, and L, rifle companies, and M, a heavy-weapons company, in the Third Battalion. I don't know why J was omitted—possibly because it sounds too much like K. That was, perhaps, the army's logic, overlooking the similarities between B, C, D, and E.

The infantry battalion included three rifle companies, a heavy-weapons company, and a headquarters company. The heavy weapons company had four 81-millimeter mortars and six heavy machine guns.

The heavy machine gun was also a .30-caliber, the M-1917. It was similar to the light machine gun. The chief difference between a light and heavy machine gun was that the heavy had a metal water jacket over the barrel, which cooled the barrel as it was being fired. The jacket and the water inside were heavy, hence, the heavy machine gun. The other difference between the two was that the heavy machine gun was mounted on a tripod that was considerably heavier than the light machine gun's bi-pod.

Appendix C

Bob Huch's First Letter from France

Dear Folks,

Back for a rest and doing fine. Feeling swell—'sep, after a little sleep and a change of clothing. Don't know how long this is going to last but will make the most of it.

I'm led to believe that back in the states, there's quite a bit of publicity about our outfit—esp. that D day affair. So, I'll try and tell you a little of what happened—with the approval of the censor, of course. I can't forget it and never will—and maybe you'll agree with me that I'm very fortunate to be here today.

Our Co. was one of a very few Co.'s in the division that made up the first wave—and I was an assault section leader— one section per assault boat. These consist of specialized equipment and a different organization, but are readily converted into the usual outfit for inland fighting. It was really a choppy sea early that morning, and all of us got soaked to the gills and seasick. It was the first time I got sick in one of those small craft—and I've spent plenty of time in those gadgets during past six months, too. Well, it was quite a long haul in, and we were all so miserable that we were anxious to get it over with. At about 800 yds off shore the shelling and machine gun fire started—with the latter bouncing off the boat making quite a racket. We then realized, by looking at the beach, that—after being promised so many tons of bombs and all from the air corps and naval support—they had all missed their mark as there was no indication that anything had hit the beach. At about 100 yds off shore, the boat hit something—it wasn't the ground, and stopped. Down went the ramp, and into five feet of water went me—followed by the section.

The machine gun fire was intense—it came from so many different directions and places, it's unbelievable. The water was deep—the only thing to do was to go in. All the way in thru the water, the bullets were splashing right in front of my nose on both sides, and everywhere right then and there I thought of every sin I committed—and never prayed so hard in my life. I just kept on going—and was firmly convinced I'd never make shore. Somehow I made it—many people didn't. Then there were obstacles all over the open beach (underwater obstacles we landed at low water) and it was about 400 yards to the high water mark, where there was a dune, about three feet high—the only cover, after leaving the boat. The only thing to do was to try to make that—which appeared impossible at the moment. The Jerry machine guns were sweeping the beach from their many pillboxes, on the high ground and emplacements. I'd advance about 30 yards and then hit the dirt, bullets going everywhere. At one point when I hit the sand, a burst went through my pack, radio, and canteen. At another point a mortar hit about 10 ft. away and the concussion knocked me out for a few seconds. Three days later I found a small piece of shrapnel in my left leg—but that didn't amount to a row of pins. Somehow I made the sea-wall, and was the first to make that spot out of either boat on our flank on my own. How, I don't know or never will. I'd look back and see the section trying to get in—and it was awful. People dying all over the place —the wounded unable to move and being drowned by the incoming tide. And boats burning madly as succeeding waves tried to get in. At least 80% of our weapons wouldn't work (my own included) because of the sand and salt water. Well, Jerry was still in the pillboxes and with shells coming in, the sea-wall wasn't the best place to be. Finally located an exit and then to clear the pillboxes. With this done, we still had to get inland considerable—and this wasn't a picnic either—Jerry was there in force.

Such was the First Division's beach. Needless to say, I lost many good men and friends—how some of us made it, we don't know. So all of your prayers and God himself took care of me. I suppose it's hard to analyze how one feels under those conditions. Scared—yes—but not mortally so. I was amazed at my own coolness and ability to think and act so clearly. And seeming ability to even joke or smile under such conditions.

Everyone I guess felt the same. I've never seen so many brave men who did so much—many would go way back and try to gather in the wounded and themselves get killed. The pleasing thing about this whole thing was that on the beach and shortly thereafter, I didn't observe one act of cowardice or hesitancy to respond to orders—not one. That's amazing—esp. so in an outfit that's been in combat previously. It's even more amazing that in all that confusion there was some order.

After that—I know I can take anything that Herman can throw at me. So don't worry about anything from here on in. We have been doing okay and will continue to do so—until he hollers "Uncle."

Well, that's out of my system—it's something I'll never forget, and every time I think about it I just wonder why I'm here. I didn't write all of this to upset or worry you—it's finished now. And I'm still mentally just about as sound as ever(?)

Also plan to enjoy this war as much as possible. Right now we can't travel about much, but Paris is something to look forward to. This land is really beautiful. Numerous shrines are all along most of the roads—I guess the people are mostly Catholic. Strangely enough, so are the Germans—practically all of the dead (and I've seen plenty of that kind) had medals and prayer books. Also have run into quite a few women snipers.

The whole business makes you stop and wonder what this is all about. It's crazy from A to Z.

Report of Captain Edward Wozenski
June 6, 1944

The following is a chronological listing of events, actions, and circumstances surrounding the landing of Co. E, 16th Inf. in the assault wave on beach "Omaha," Easy Red, north of Colleville Sur Mer, France on 6 June 1944.

Aboard the U.S.S. Henrico - APA #2. Reveille was sounded at 01:00 hrs. Quarters were policed and equipment collected and adjusted for debarkation.

Details from the company reported to the ship's galley for breakfast which consisted of black coffee and one sandwich per man, not a very appetizing mess.

At 03:00 hrs., Co. E. was called to debarkation stations.

At 04:15 hrs., the assault wave was lowered into the sea, which was very rough for the small assault craft. There was considerable milling about, shouting, and jockeying for positions on the part of the assault craft until they were in proper order for rendezvousing. The order to lower away was delayed for some reason and the assault craft were considerably knocked about by banging into the mother ship as she rolled in the heavy seas.

Once in the rendezvous area, as in many of our prior exercises, there was the usual racing about for well over an hour during which every man was soaked and many sickened.

With H-hour at 06:30 hrs., apprehension increased as we continued to rendezvous after 06:00 hrs. At approximately 06:00 hrs., heavy naval support weapons opened up with their fiery display, followed by flashes from the distant shore, where the shells were landing. A few enemy planes floated over the massed invasion forces, dropping their long burning flares.

Anxious eyes scanned the dawn lightened skies, searching for the hundreds of promised bombers—especially any headed for "EASY RED," our beach. Damn few were seen, and these were mainly high flying fighters.

Now we were headed in for shore—pounding in the rough seas. Out to our front we could see the LCR's moving up to firing positions. Guide craft and tank ships were out front as well as small support boats. About a mile off shore, we began to pass a few, and then more and more men tossing about in the water in life belts and small rubber rafts. At first we thought these men were shot down airmen but soon realized they must be tank men from tanks that had sunk from the heavy sea.

We knew our timetable was off when, as we were still 10-15 minutes off shore, the rocket ships opened up with their thousands of rockets. It certainly was an impressive and cheering sight. Unfortunately as a was later seen, it was morale effect only that was achieved by our rocket ships, for we saw no material effects of their landing—all had fallen into the water.

Absolutely nothing was seen of the assault craft from the 116th Inf. to our right. We didn't know if they had already landed or were still out of sight behind us. Nearing the shore to a point where it was possible to easily recognize landmarks, it became obvious that the company was being landed approximately 1000 yds. left of the scheduled landing point. How anyone who had been briefed could make such an error, I will never know, for the lone house which so prominently marked Exit #3 was in flames, and clearly showed its distinctive outline.

Small arms and anti-tank fire opened up on us as we were still 500-600 yds off shore. When told to fire back from our LCVP with the machine guns mounted astern, the naval man on one gun fired a burst straight up into the air, as he hid his head below the deck—a disgusting performance if I ever saw one. No one would man the second machine gun.

Machine gun fire was rattling against the ramp as the boat grounded. For some reason the ramp would not go down. Four or five men battered at the ramp until if finally fell, and the men with it. The boats were hurriedly emptied - the men jumping into water shoulder high, under intense machine gun and anti-tank fire. No sooner was the last man out than the boat received two direct hits and blew up and burned.

Now, all the men in the company could be seen wading ashore into the face of intense fire from the machine guns, rifles, anti-tank guns and mortars. Due to the heavy sea, the strong cross current, and the loads that the men were carrying, no one could run. It was just a slow methodical march with absolutely no cover up to the enemy's commanding positions. Many fell left and right and the water reddened with their blood. A few men hit underwater mines of some sort and were blown out of the sea. The others staggered on to the obstacle covered, yet completely exposed beach. Here men in sheer exhaustion hit the beach, only to rise and move forward through a tide runlet that threatened to sweep them off their feet. Men were falling on all sides, but the survivors still moved forward and eventually worked up to a pile of shale at the high water mark. This offered momentary protection against the murderous fire of the close-in enemy guns, but his mortars were still raising hell.

A firing line was built up along this pile of shale, and the enemy guns were brought under small arms' fire. Unfortunately most of our guns were jammed with sand, but every arm was brought to bear on the enemy. Men armed with pistols alone were firing back at machine guns, in an effort to cover the company's men still struggling ashore. Other men displaying the best in courage and devotion to duty, stripped and cleaned their weapons while under heavy fire. Though enemy fire and snipers would mercilessly mow down anyone attempting to go back to the water and drag their wounded comrades up to the lee of the shale, many men dropped back to do it, and a few succeeded despite the point-blank enemy fire.

An attempt was made to reorganize the scattered remnants of the company for an attack on the enemy strong-point to our front. Only ten men could be found and most of their weapons were jammed. All radio communication was gone. An attempt to get smoke for cover was made, but without avail.

Finally in an effort to reorganize in some strength, a lateral movement along the exposed beach was started. Men were picked up in scattered intervals, as we headed towards our original landing point to our right.

Approaching this point, it was seen that the 1st platoon, Co. E had broken through just east of exit #1. There, Lt. Spaulding with his platoon made the initial breakthrough from the beach, and the entire beach "Easy Red" was attempting to clear inland by his route despite the fact that it was being swept by machine gun, artillery, and mortar fire. Mines were thickly sown throughout the area, but the company heedless of this danger, realized the necessity of a breakthrough, and plunged boldly through to attack and silence the machine guns covering this sector.

Working their way up to the top of the high ground overlooking the beach, the 1st platoon, under covering fire from the rest of the company, worked west where the strong point was reduced—pillbox by pillbox, overlooking the east side of exit #1. Extremely stubborn resistance was encountered in this strong point, with its maze of underground shelters, trenches, and dugouts. There was a close exchange of grenades and small arms' fire until the platoon had cornered about twenty men and an officer. Again there was a fierce exchange of grenades in the confined trenches, until the enemy was overpowered and surrendered.

Having cleaned up this strong point, the remnants of the company, without communication of any kind, pushed on towards its objective. Reaching a point about 1,000 yds. south of E#1, the company was help up and partially reorganized. A rough check showed that well over 100 men out of the 183 that landed were killed, wounded, or missing. Patrols were sent into a newly discovered strong-point to our front, until the 1st Bn. took over the job of reducing it.

Orders came from Bn. by runner to move east toward Colleville Sur Mer. The company moved east, then south along the road towards the town. Snipers were extremely active throughout, but the company moved onto its destination. Heavy artillery fire registered on the company but no casualties were suffered.

The Bn. comdr ordered the company, then about 50 strong, to sweep the woods and fields west of the Colleville road and proceed to the Colleville-St. Laurent Road. The company swept forward without serious opposition, but the small hdqts group following the deployed company was repeatedly pinned down by machine gun and sniper fire. It became evident that the enemy was not firing on large groups but was concentrating on small groups. The enemy had previously prepared foxholes, trenches and deadly fields of fire throughout this area and was difficult to locate and drive off.

"G" Co., 2nd Bn., 16th Inf., had in the meantime moved up to Colleville Sur Mer and occupied the west half of the town in a bitter struggle. "E" Co., with an attachment of one section of "H" Co. machine guns, was given the mission of building up the Bn. line by going in to cover "G" Company's right flank, which was exposed to numerous enemy machine guns and machine-pistol men.

Two skeleton sections of the company moved up under Lt. Robert A. Huch to take positions on the right of "G" Co. The situation at the time was extremely touch and go, with the enemy in front, amongst, and behind us. Still Lt. Huch led his men into this rather desperate situation where, by setting himself up and holding his ground, he eased the dangerous pressure on "G" Company's right and eventually established a Bn. line to be held until a reorganization was effected the next day. Though completely surrounded many times, knowing that no supporting troops were nearby, and without any communications of any kind, the company held this ground throughout the critical night and, by morning, had sufficiently reorganized both its personnel and position to repel enemy thrusts and insure the success of the beachhead in our particular sector.

So ended the period H to H plus 24 hrs 6 June 1944 for Company "E," 16th Infantry.

Signed Edward F. Wozenski
Capt. 16th Inf.
Commanding

Glossary

Definitions of Military Terms

Approach March - The military formation that an infantry unit is in while advancing toward the enemy but before contacting the enemy. An approach march for a rifle squad is a column of the twelve-man squad with its two scouts in the lead to give warning if the attack or defend by forming a skirmish line in which the men spread from a column to a line with all men abreast with each other facing the enemy.

B-24 - A World War II American heavy bomber. It had four engines, was known as the Liberator and is most easily identified by its twin tail fins.

BAR - Browning automatic rifle. The .30 caliber automatic rifle used by the American Army in World War II.

Bazooka - An anti-tank weapon utilized by both the German and American armies in World War II. It was a hollow metal tube about four feet long that rested on the shoulder of the man firing it and was loaded by a second man by inserting a rocket through the rear of the tube. When the firer had the target (usually a tank) in his sights, he would press the trigger, and the rocket would be ejected towards the target. The rocket would not be propelled by an explosion like in an artillery shell or rifle round, but by the thrust generated within the rocket after it was fired. The advantage of a bazooka over an anti-tank gun was that two men could carry and fire a projectile as powerful as a 75 millimeter anti-tank gun that required several men to operate and maneuver.

Blitzkrieg - Lightning war. The German word describing the operations of the German armies early in World War II. They drove with skill and speed and power to overrun first Poland and later Denmark, Norway, Belgium, the Netherlands, Luxembourg, and France. To civilians of the times (1939 and 1940), the Germans were unbeatable.

Bouncing Betty - The name the American soldiers gave to the German anti-personnel mine designated the S-1 by the Germans. When a soldier stepped on it, it would spring up into the air to a height of a man and then explode and hurl dozens of pieces of sharp shrapnel or ball bearings in all directions, wounding any nearby American soldiers. See Chapter Seven for further discussion.

Burp Gun - The German MP-40. An automatic machine pistol carried by many German infantrymen. In combat, I heard them often. They would be fired in short bursts, showing the German soldiers' lack of the niceties of polite society, sounding distinctly like bur-urp, bur-urp, bur-urp.

C.O. - Commanding officer. The person in charge of a military unit, including an army, corps, division, brigade, regiment, battalion, and company. But, in the smallest units, the platoon, section, and squad, that person was called the "leader," not the C.O.

C.P. - Command post. The place where the commander of a unit was located. For example, the C.P. of a rifle company was where the company commander stayed. In combat, it was either in a foxhole or in the basement of an abandoned building. He would have with him his radio man with radios, probably the first sergeant, and, if there was room, perhaps others. He might even have had a kerosene lamp, an instrument which men in rifle platoons considered to be the height of luxury.

Esprit de Corps - Literally, French for "the spirit of the body or group." It is defined in the *American Heritage Dictionary of the English Language* as, "a common spirit of devotion and enthusiasm among members of a group." As a former front-line infantryman, there was never any sign of enthusiasm among my peers to risk our lives fighting the enemy. The only common spirit of enthusiasm was for such things as a cold bottle of beer on a hot summer day. For a further discussion of esprit de corps, see Chapter Eight.

Forward Observer - The man in the front lines with the infantry who would direct or "call" the fire for the artillery or mortars, which were, of course, behind the front lines. See Chapter Four for an example of an incompetent forward observer.

GIs - The GI Shits. GI - government issue. The soldier's euphemism for diarrhea, a common malady occurring in combat. To a front-line infantryman huddling in a foxhole for survival during an artillery barrage, the sudden onset of the GIs was a real problem. See Chapter Six and Seven for my experience with the GIs.

Latrine - The army's word for lavatory.

M-1 - The American .30 caliber semi-automatic rifle carried by the infantry. It was also called the Garand for the man who invented it. In the twelve-man rifle squad, eleven men carried the M-1 while one carried the automatic rifle. M-1 was the appellation assigned by the U.S. Army to other weapons as well as to equipment, such as the gas mask. But when an infantryman heard the word M-1, he thought of the rifle, not the gas mask.

Non-coms - Non-commissioned officers, corporals and sergeants.

P.F.C. - Private First Class.

P-38 - A World War II American fighter plane. It was known as the Lightening and was most easily identified by its twin fuselage. Another P-38 was a pistol carried by the Germans in World War II. It was similar in appearance to the better known and highly prized Luger. I once took a P-38 from a German prisoner and, after the shooting was over, was quite disappointed that it was not a Luger.

Panzerfaust - A German anti-tank projectile that was similar to a rocket with a large explosive charge attached to its front. Like a bazooka, it was carried and fired by one man. (The bazooka required a second man to carry and load the rockets.) Unlike the bazooka, however, the panzerfaust was fired once and discarded.

Potato Masher - A German hand grenade shaped like an old-fashioned potato masher (a kitchen utensil used to mash potatoes). It had a foot-long wooden handle with the explosive element at the end of the handle. See Chapter Six for my close affinity with the potato masher.

ROTC - Reserve Officers Training Corps. The program was sponsored by the U.S. military and trained young candidates to be army officers. The ROTC members were students in high schools and colleges. Upon graduation and completing the army's summer camp after their junior year, the students received a commission as a second lieutenant in the Army Reserve.

Shavetail - "A newly commissioned officer: Second Lieutenant, usually used disparagingly"—*Webster's Third New International Dictionary of the English Language, Unabridged*. When they came up with that definition, I think they had in mind someone like a young man I knew well. In fact, I was with him through his, and my, army career. But he shall remain nameless.

Skirmish Line - The military formation in which the men in an infantry unit, such as a rifle squad of twelve men, would be spread out abreast of each other facing the enemy, forming what might be called a firing line.

Springfield - The M1903 Springfield rifle. This was the .30 caliber, bolt-action rifle carried by the American infantry in World War I. The drawback to a bolt action rifle was that the bolt must be pulled back and pushed forward after every shot, thereby greatly reducing the rate of fire. The M-1, a semi-automatic rifle, which did not have this drawback, replaced the Springfield in World War II.

Strategy - In a military sense, strategy is the overall and broad planning of military operations. The details of an operation are considered tactics. The decision for the allied armies to carry out the D-Day landings in Normandy is strategy. The details as to how those landings were to be carried out is tactics.

Tactics - In a military sense, tactics is the detailed plan by which a military unit attacks or defends against an enemy. See further discussion under "Strategy." Keeping in mind the confusion and disarray that often pervade during infantry actions, a more descriptive phrase, rather than "tactics," might be "muddling along."

Wehrmacht - The German armed forces.

Index

About the Author

William "Bill" Devitt was born in St. Paul, Minnesota, on May 25, 1923. He graduated from St. Thomas Military Academy (now St. Thomas Academy) in 1941. As a result of his St. Thomas training, he received in 1943 a commission as a second lieutenant in the U.S. Army. He served in the army in World War II from 1943 to 1946 and in the Korean Conflict for seventeen months. After his military service, he received from the University of Minnesota degrees in business administration and law. He practiced law from 1955 to 1988 when he retired. About 1990, he started work on this book and completed it in 2001. He is a slow worker. He married Mary McNulty in 1952. They have eight children  and fourteen grandchildren. Mary and Bill presently have one house, one car, one lawn mower, and eleven sets of dishes.